National Trust
SOUPS

National Trust

SOUPS

80 tasty, easy and thrifty recipes

Maggie Ramsay

Published by National Trust Books

An imprint of HarperCollins Publishers, 1 London Bridge Street London SE1 9GF
www.harpercollins.co.uk

HarperCollins Publishers, Macken House, 39/40 Mayor Street Upper,
Dublin 1, D01 C9W8, Ireland

First published 2023
© National Trust Books 2023
Text © Maggie Ramsay 2023
Illustrations © Astrid Weguelin 2023

ISBN 978-0-00-860433-2

10 9 8 7 6 5 4 3 2 1

The contents of this publication are believed correct at the time of printing. Nevertheless, the
publisher can accept no responsibility for errors or omissions, changes in the detail given or for any
expense or loss thereby caused.

A catalogue record for this book is available from the British Library.
Printed and bound in Slovenia

If you would like to comment on any aspect of this book, please contact us at the above address or
national.trust@harpercollins.co.uk

National Trust publications are available at National Trust shops or online at nationaltrustbooks.co.uk

This book is produced from independently certified FSC™ paper
to ensure responsible forest management.

For more information visit: www.harpercollins.co.uk/green

Contents

Introduction

Soup is the original one-pot wonder. In its myriad forms it has sustained humans for thousands of years. Out of the cooking pot appears a whole cast of characters, led by big, hearty soups packed with vegetables, pulses or pasta, and often topped with yogurt or cheese – soups such as minestrone, goulash or scotch broth. As a first course, soup can be an elegant, well-flavoured clear broth or a robust, spicy extravaganza with an array of imaginative garnishes. Chilled soups and fruit soups make delightful, refreshing starters and desserts. In a traditional Chinese banquet, soup is sipped as a drink throughout the meal. And in some countries soup is eaten for breakfast: it's filling, high in nutrients and low in sugar, ideal to get you through the morning. In a vacuum flask, soup is the traveller's friend. And Doctor Soup is called in to ward off illness and to soothe the sick and convalescent.

Inspired by soups from around the world, I explore in this book the ways in which soup works its comforting magic. For some of us, it's that warming hug in a bowl that brings back childhood memories of being cared for. And there's no doubt that soup is nourishing, as the gentle cooking makes it easy to digest and retains nutrients in the broth. The restorative power of soup gave rise to the word 'restaurant': in Paris in the 1760s some new establishments served light dishes, including *bouillon restaurant*, or 'restorative broth', in contrast to the heavier food found in the taverns; these establishments became known as restaurants. You're sure to find a restorative soup on the menu at the National Trust's cafés. Soup is always a popular choice: it's the perfect way to fill up before exploring a historic house or to refuel after a coastal or country walk. Some of the soups in this book are inspired by recipes developed by the National Trust chefs to make the most of fresh, seasonal vegetables.

Some studies have found that soup, made with a very small amount of fat, has a satiating effect, helping us to feel full for longer, which is why a bowl of soup makes such a satisfying lunch or supper. The message is loud and clear that, for good health, we should all be eating more plants and less meat, and soups can play an important part. It's easy to pack vegetables into soup, and even if you're not keen on spinach, kale or cabbage, they can be 'hidden' when blended into soup. An interesting new message is emerging, based on research into the bacteria (microbes) that live in our gut. These bacteria have a number of functions, such as producing anti-inflammatory substances and supporting our immune system to keep us healthy. They thrive on plant-based foods, and it appears that diversity is important too. The goal is to eat at least 30 different plant-based foods a week. Why not start a list and see how close you get? Each item counts only once in the week, but the good news is that it's not just fresh fruit and veg but all plants, including whole grains, pulses, dried fruits, spices – and the herbs, nuts and seeds that look so good scattered on your soup. As well as brightening up your plate, that herb garnish is also giving your hard-working gut bacteria a bonus.

Versatile and nutritious, soup is one of the easiest things that anyone can make, with just one pan simmering on the hob and no worries about oven timings and temperatures. In summer, you don't even need to turn on the heat to make a refreshing gazpacho (page 132) or creamy cucumber soup (page 136). Soup is also one of the most economical of dishes. With a seasonal glut of home-grown veg or an end-of-the-day bargain from the supermarket, a garden vegetable soup (page 28) is a bowlful of goodness that you can make at any time of year. Freeze vegetables as they are,

Sustainability

Avoiding food waste is a powerful tool to protect the planet. It's not just the fact that so much food ends up in landfill, emitting millions of tonnes of greenhouse gases, but we should also consider the massive waste of water, energy and human resources used in growing and transporting food. Being mindful of how much we buy, storing it wisely and using leftovers to make another meal – such as soup – are simple steps that we can all take.

Avoiding excessive packaging is not always so easy, especially when shopping online, but awareness of such issues helps us to make more informed decisions when buying food. Reducing food miles by eating only foods produced locally, perhaps within a 50- or 100-mile radius, is something our ancestors would recognise, but let's not forget that pepper, cinnamon and other spices have been imported for a thousand years, and lemons, other exotic fruit and nuts for almost as long. It's not just a matter of food miles. Seasonality is more important than we may realise. Producing crops all year round is often the result of unnatural farming practices, such as excessive irrigation and the use of synthetic fertilisers, pesticides and herbicides, which have a drastic effect on biodiversity as well as polluting rivers and groundwater.

Eating more vegetables and pulses while reducing our consumption of meat and poultry can make a positive contribution to the future of the planet, but not everyone is thrilled at the idea of going completely vegan. With good farming practices, cows, sheep and pigs can contribute to improving soil health and increasing biodiversity. Sustainable eating can mean respecting the animals that feed us by using every part, including less tender cuts such as beef shin, lamb neck, ham hock: the traditional ingredients of slow-cooked soups and stews. With today's energy-efficient slow cookers and pressure cookers we can return to these cheaper cuts while also economising on fuel.

or make them into soup and then freeze – either way you'll be following ancient traditions of preserving produce to enjoy during the leaner months.

Reducing food waste is another of soup's superpowers. It's perfect for using oddly shaped and slightly blemished vegetables (just trim out any discoloured bits), outer leaves and stalks (slice them thinly), and all kinds of leftovers. Get creative and conjure up a new dish from the food in your fridge, freezer or cupboard, adding spices, sauces or herbs. As a starting point, see Boxing Day Soup (page 97) and Ribollita (page 80). If your leftovers – cooked or raw – aren't enough to make a soup on their own, why not try combining ingredients: leek and sweet potato; courgette and watercress; celeriac and fennel?

Choosing a (more) plant-based diet is good for our health and that of our planet. More than half of the recipes in this book are vegetarian or vegan, reflecting the history of soup – particularly its early days as 'pottage': the everyday food of the majority of the population of medieval Europe. Based on grains and dried legumes (peas, lentils, chickpeas and broad beans) in poorer households, its flavour varied little throughout the year. However, it was warming and filling, and in different seasons it might have included garlic, onions, leeks, kale and cabbages, roots (such as turnips, carrots and parsnips), wild or cultivated herbs, leaves and seeds and – whenever it was available – a small amount of meat, usually salted pork or bacon. At the other end of the social scale, meat or fowl would have been the main ingredient, with ground nuts and spices to add variety. Today, soup can be as frugal or as decadent as you choose. Onion soup, for example, is made from the most basic ingredients, but with a generous plate of cheese toasts it becomes a feast (page 45).

In this collection of recipes you'll find classics such as Asparagus Soup (page 24) and Scottish Cullen Skink (page 125), rediscovered 'peasant' soups such as Portuguese Caldo Verde (page 20) and Nettle Soup (page 22), and contemporary twists on Cream of Chicken Soup (page 88) and Chilled Tomato and Basil Soup (page 139). I've reinterpreted soups such as Miso Ramen (page 67) and Laksa (page 70) to cut out the meat and fish, and adapted traditional recipes to reduce the fat, pack in more vegetables or shorten cooking times. I hope you'll enjoy making them and finding some new favourites.

How to Make Soup

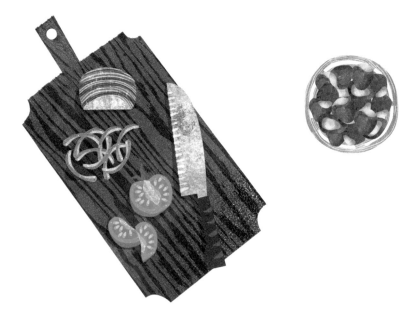

Equipment

No special equipment is needed for soup making: it's one of the earliest cooking techniques, and all you really need is a knife, a chopping board and a big pot or saucepan. As most soups need gentle simmering, a large saucepan with a heavy base helps to keep the temperature even without burning the ingredients at the bottom of the pan. That said, many of the soups in this book are blended (but see below for more about blending).

- A vegetable peeler is, for most cooks, far easier than peeling with a knife; however, instead of peeling root veg you can scrub them, which avoids wasting the nutrients just below the skin (use a small sharp knife to nick out any blemishes), so you'll need a vegetable scrubbing brush.

- I couldn't be without my (digital) kitchen scales, measuring spoons and a large heatproof measuring jug, nor my flexible rubber spatula, which I always use to scrape every drop of soup out of the pan.

- A colander is used for draining vegetables and a fine mesh sieve for straining stock. Serving soup is a lot quicker if you use a ladle.

- Some recipes call for ingredients to be ground to a powder or paste. For this you'll need a pestle and mortar or an electric spice grinder, blender, mini chopper or food processor.

- A mezzaluna makes it quick and easy to finely chop herbs, but it is certainly not essential.

- The best pan for making stock is the classic stockpot: it's tall and narrow to avoid evaporation, with a tight-fitting lid and side handles for stability. It needn't be heavy-based, as it's used over a low heat, and you don't want a pot that's too heavy to lift when it's full of liquid: 4–5 litres is a good size for most kitchens. Again, it's not essential, as you can use your largest saucepan.

- I often use a pressure cooker to speed up stock-making and when long cooking times are needed for beans and certain cuts of meat. A slow cooker is another energy-efficient alternative.

Blending

Many soups have a smooth, creamy texture as a result of blending some or all of the ingredients. Either a jug blender or a hand-held stick blender will do the job.

Every source I've consulted gives a warning about the potential danger of blending soup in a jug blender: if the soup is too hot, or you try to blend too much at a time, or you don't hold the blender lid down *before starting the machine*, you risk getting painfully splattered with hot soup. To sum up, then, if you use a jug blender:

- Leave the soup to cool for 5–10 minutes before blending.

- Blend the soup in batches, filling the blender about halfway each time. This means that you will need to transfer the blended soup to another container while you blend the remaining soup. If you remember, first rinse the container with boiling water from the kettle to help keep the blended soup warm.

- Hold the lid of the blender down firmly – you may want to cover the top with a tea towel – and pulse the soup a few times. Steam will build up (and try to push the lid off), so take the lid off to let the steam out, then replace it and start blending.

A hand-held stick blender avoids these problems, as it is used directly in the soup pan. Keep it at the bottom of the pan to avoid splashes, moving it around gently and switching it off every so often to scrape down the sides of the pan with a rubber spatula.

Before electric blenders were commonplace, if cooks wanted a puréed soup, they had to rub the solids through a sieve. The *mouli-légumes* (food mill) was invented in France in the 1930s and soon found its way around the world. Several generations of cooks have used the *mouli* for soups, sauces and vegetable purées – but not in my family, and my grandmother was a superb cook. In some recipes, such as asparagus soup, I recommend rubbing the soups through a fine sieve to remove the fibrous bits of vegetable for a really smooth result.

Note that soups don't always need to be blended until completely smooth: it's often nice to leave some of the soup unblended, to vary the texture.

Techniques

Making soup is not a science, but an art – and a very forgiving art. The recipes in this book should be considered as a starting point. Ingredients, especially vegetables, vary enormously and may give slightly different results, but with most of the hot soups I've aimed for about 300ml (10½fl oz) per person. If you want to make the soup go further, it's a simple matter of adding a little more of the main ingredient and liquid – or add other vegetables or pulses for variety, if you prefer. Chilled soups are generally served in smaller portions.

As a rough guide, these are the weights I've used in testing:

1 large onion 200g (7oz)+	1 large potato 250–350g (9–12oz)
1 medium onion 140–190g (5–6¾oz)	1 medium potato 150–240g (5½–8½oz)
1 small onion 85–130g (3–4¾oz)	1 small potato 70–140g (2½–5oz)

Mostly, I'm assuming that you'll use 'medium' vegetables – meaning whatever's available. If an onion, carrot or potato is small, use two.

It's important to read the recipe all the way through before starting. Check that you have all the equipment and ingredients (or make the decision to swap or leave something out) and think about prep: you'll save time and fluster by weighing and chopping before you start cooking, although there may be some things you can do while another stage is under way. Scrubbing veg and prepping ingredients can be a mindful activity, and setting out everything in advance results in a serene feeling that once you start cooking it will be plain sailing.

In the recipes, I've given timings for most stages of cooking, but it's more important to use your senses to check whether vegetables are tender – which might depend on their variety, age and how small you cut them.

If you have a spare half hour, make up some 'soup base mix' for the freezer. With this, you'll be able to whip up almost any soup with impressive chef-like ease. Finely chop onions and freeze. Alternatively make an Italian-style mix of onion, carrot and celery, known as *soffritto*: finely dice equal quantities of onions, carrots and celery, and freeze for up to 2 months. Cook from frozen.

Basic vegetable soup to serve 1

½ tbsp vegetable oil, or use butter, bacon fat, dripping
    from roast beef, or the fat from roasted poultry

1 onion, chopped, or leek, sliced, or a bunch of spring
    onions, sliced

Garlic, spices, or herbs such as thyme, sage or
    rosemary (optional)

200g (7oz) vegetables (see Tip), chopped into
    small pieces

250ml (9fl oz) stock or water

Salt and pepper

Chopped fresh herbs such as chives, basil, tarragon
    or parsley (optional), to serve

Heat the oil in a large saucepan over a medium heat. Add the onion and a pinch of salt, and cook for 10 minutes or until well softened, stirring from time to time.

Add the garlic, herbs or spices, if using, and stir for a few minutes to coat them in the onion mix. Add the vegetables to the pan.

Add the stock or water and bring to the boil, then turn down the heat so that the soup simmers gently but steadily until the vegetables are tender. (Maximise the flavour and nutritional benefits by cooking the veg for as short a time as possible: just as long as it takes for them to be cooked through and tender enough to be blended.)

Taste the soup and adjust the seasoning. (Don't forget this step, or your soup will be disappointing.)

If you like, blend the soup partly, or until completely smooth. Add a little boiling water if it is too thick. Stir in fresh herbs, if using, or sprinkle them over the finished soup.

Tip

If you like your soup to have a certain thickness, it's a good idea to include a small potato, unless your chosen vegetable is a starchy one such as sweet potato, squash, tinned beans or cooked pulses.

Seasoning

Soups should be seasoned generously but carefully. If you add a little salt at various stages of cooking, you shouldn't need to add much to the finished soup. Some ingredients, such as bacon and shellfish, are naturally high in salt, whereas other ingredients, such as herbs, have prominent flavours that call for judicious seasoning. Ready-made stock – especially if made from stock cubes or bouillon powder – can be excessively salty, so taste it before you begin to add it: you may need to dilute it with more boiling water. I tend to use twice the amount of water suggested on the pack of bouillon powder or stock cubes. I use freshly ground black pepper, mostly added near the end of cooking to enjoy its aromatic spiciness.

Some of the soups have less chilli heat than you might expect: this is partly to make them more family friendly, and partly because chillies vary enormously in their spicy heat. I find it best to go low, adding just enough chilli for flavour and warmth. I admit to being a chilli wimp, so you could offer chilli lovers a bottle of sriracha or Tabasco to drizzle into their bowl.

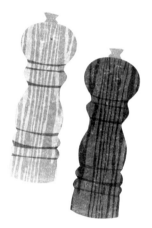

Thickening

Arguably, the most sophisticated of the classic European soups is consommé, an unthickened, crystal-clear, intensely flavoured broth. It starts off as a well-flavoured stock made from bones (traditionally veal, chicken or game), gently simmered for several hours to extract the maximum amount of gelatine, before being clarified with additional ingredients to boost the flavour and catch impurities. The gelatine (derived from collagen in the bones) gives the broth body and, if chilled, it will set to a jelly, which can be served as a first course for a summer dinner party.

At the other end of the spectrum are the bread-thickened soups such as French onion, Spanish gazpacho and Tuscan ribollita. Until relatively recently these were considered soups to fill the bellies of workers, never seen on the tables of the better off. Times change.

One of the easiest ways to thicken a soup – especially if you have a stick blender – is to purée some of the vegetables, pulses or grains that have been cooked in the stock.

Starchy elements such as rice, pasta and potatoes, when cooked in a soup, will have a slight thickening effect, or you can sprinkle a little flour over the softened vegetable base, cooking it for a few minutes before gradually adding the liquid: this method is used for the Clam Chowder on page 120.

For last-minute thickening, mix a little cornflour or arrowroot with cold water until smooth, then stir it into the soup and simmer for 2–3 minutes until thickened – once you've done this, the soup should be served straight away.

Another way to thicken soups at the last minute now seems rather luxurious, but it gives a rich and delicate finish. The soup should be seasoned and ready to serve, but below boiling point. Whisk 2 egg yolks in a small

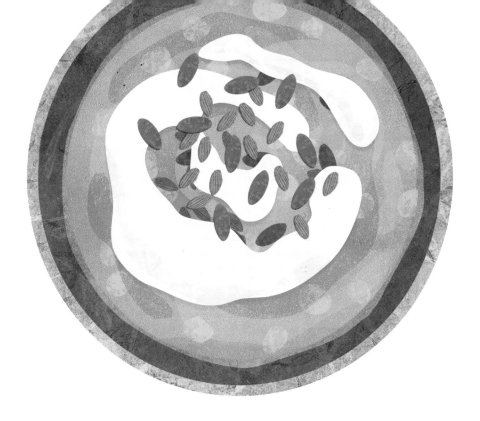

bowl, then gradually whisk in about 100ml (3½fl oz) (a ladleful) of the hot soup. Whisk the mixture back into the soup, ensuring that it doesn't boil, or the eggs will curdle.

Storing

Most of the recipes can easily be halved if you're cooking for one or two. Alternatively, if you have a big enough pan, you can make double quantities and refrigerate or freeze what you don't need.

Freeze soup in individual servings on the day you make it for a no-fuss supper at a later date: most soups freeze well – without their garnish – for two or three months. Defrost and reheat over a medium heat, without boiling, until piping hot. Stir regularly while reheating.

Many soups improve if made a day or two ahead and kept in a covered container in the fridge. Reheat as above. If serving soup two days in a row, think about giving it a new look with a different garnish (see page 151), or simply refresh the flavour with some freshly ground black pepper, a squeeze of lemon or lime juice, a dash of soy sauce, balsamic vinegar, chilli flakes, chilli sauce or a sprinkling of fresh herbs.

Soup Up Your Veg

Vegetable soups are a simple and delicious way to celebrate the seasons. When summer is in full swing there's a riot of colourful vegetables to choose from: green beans, lettuces, courgettes, fennel and fragrant ripe tomatoes – not forgetting fresh herbs. Moving into autumn we find sweetcorn, peppers, squashes and the first of the root vegetables. Leeks, cabbage and kale are traditional winter greens, as they continue to grow in cold and frosty weather to be harvested when needed. Onions, potatoes and other roots and tubers can be stored in cool conditions for several months. By March, however, veg stocks would traditionally have been running low, and the appearance of green shoots such as wild garlic, nettles and other wild greens was welcomed in spring, heralding the asparagus to follow.

Vegetable growers can now choose varieties with extended growing seasons, and we are fortunate to have a wide range of produce in our shops and markets. But given the choice between air-freighted, plastic-wrapped, out-of-season veg and bouncy-fresh produce grown in its natural season, the latter wins every time – for flavour, our health and the health of our planet. That said, frozen vegetables are an invaluable standby, helping us to whip up a soup at short notice, and foods that are frozen within hours of being harvested are often richer in nutrients and flavour than fresh versions that have sat in the shop for a week.

The nutritional benefits of soup are hard to ignore. A bowl of vegetable soup may contain two or more of the recommended daily minimum of five portions of fruit and veg. The 'five-a-day' campaign has been fine-tuned over the years, with advice to 'eat the rainbow' (by choosing different-coloured fruit and veg), aim for ten a day, or follow the recent suggestion of eating 30 different plant-based foods a week (see pages 6–7). As well as vitamins, minerals and fibre, vegetables and fruit contain various phytochemicals (the term for a huge number of compounds produced by plants), all of which interact with each other within our bodies to keep us healthy. Long-term benefits include reducing the risk of heart disease, stroke, diabetes and many types of cancer, promoting healthy eyesight, preventing anaemia and building strong bones. Increasing our vegetable intake can also reduce stress and help us to feel more positive every day.

Vegetable soup is easy to make (see page 13) and extremely versatile: with a base of onions, leeks, shallots or spring onions, you can add just about any vegetable and produce a satisfying meal. Using whatever veg is available is a great way to save money, avoid food waste and support farmers, who have invested so much in growing their crops. Homemade soup is also much cheaper than any ready-made version. In this chapter you'll find soups for all seasons.

Watercress Soup

Serves **4**
Prep **15 mins**
Cook **25 mins**

V Vegetarian
GF Gluten-free

Gloriously green, bursting with vitamins, iron, calcium and magnesium, watercress also boasts a wealth of plant compounds with an impressive list of health benefits. It's available all year round, so it's particularly welcome in early spring, when winter vegetables are coming to an end before the new season's crops are ready.

30g (1oz) butter

1 large onion, chopped

350g (12oz) potatoes, diced

800ml (28fl oz) vegetable stock, chicken stock or hot water

250g (9oz) watercress, roughly chopped

4 tbsp double cream, plus extra to serve (optional)

Salt and pepper

Melt the butter in a saucepan over a low heat, add the onion and a pinch of salt, and cook for 8–10 minutes until softened.

Add the potatoes and stir to coat in the buttery onions, then add the stock and bring to the boil. Reduce the heat, cover and simmer for 15 minutes or until the potato is tender.

Add the watercress (reserving some leaves to garnish, if you like) and bring back to the boil over a high heat, then immediately remove from the heat.

Blitz the soup with a stick blender until smooth, then taste and season with salt and pepper.

Stir in the cream and gently reheat. Serve hot, garnished, if you like, with a swirl of cream and a few watercress leaves.

Tips

- Croutons (page 156) or a bright nasturtium flower would raise the presentation stakes. To add an intriguing flavour, serve with a slice of Blue Cheese Butter (page 153) melting into the hot soup.
- If you like, whip an extra 4 tablespoons of double cream and float on top of the soup. Alternatively, add a small spoonful of crème fraîche.
- Wild garlic or sorrel soup: replace the watercress with 170–200g (6–7oz), about four good handfuls, of wild garlic or sorrel leaves.

Carrot, Orange and Coriander Soup

Serves   **4**
Prep   **10 mins**
Cook   **40–50 mins**

 Vegan

GF Gluten-free

This comforting carrot soup is easy to make and glowing with goodness. Adapted from a recipe created by the National Trust chefs, it uses the stalks as well as the leaves of fresh coriander. Adding fresh orange juice just before blending lends a vibrant citrus note. The new season's carrots appear in late spring, but carrots are harvested through to autumn and they store well, so they can add colour to soups all year round.

2 tbsp vegetable oil

1 large onion, chopped

2 tsp ground coriander

600g (1lb 5oz) carrots, chopped

A good handful of fresh coriander, stalks separated and chopped

Grated zest and juice of 1 orange

100g (3½oz) basmati rice

1 litre (1¾ pints) vegetable stock

Salt and pepper

Croutons (page 156) or Toasted Seeds (page 158) (optional), to serve

Heat the oil in a saucepan over a medium heat, add the onion and a pinch of salt, and cook for 8–10 minutes until softened.

Add the ground coriander, carrots, chopped coriander stalks, orange zest and another pinch of salt, and cook for a further 10 minutes.

Add the rice, stock and a good grinding of pepper and bring to the boil. Reduce the heat, cover and simmer for 20–30 minutes until the rice and carrots are soft.

Leave to cool slightly, then add the orange juice and half the coriander leaves. Blitz the soup with a stick blender until smooth. Taste and adjust the seasoning. Reheat if needed.

Serve sprinkled with the remaining coriander leaves, plus croutons or toasted seeds, if you like.

Caldo Verde

Serves **4–6**
Prep **20 mins**
Cook **20 mins**

A rustic Portuguese soup of potatoes with kale, *caldo verde* means 'green broth'. The kale is very finely shredded (so that it looks like grass) and the soup is served with a few slices of chorizo (*chouriço* in Portuguese). As in many cuisines around the world, a small amount of meat is traditionally included to boost the flavour of the vegetables. Kale is a hardy plant that can be grown at any time of year, so it's a vital source of greenery in times of the year when there's not much else around.

4 floury potatoes (see Tip), about 600g (1lb 5oz), cut into chunks

½ small onion, chopped

1 garlic clove, chopped

200g (7oz) kale or spring greens

85g (3oz) chorizo, sliced

2 tbsp extra virgin olive oil, plus extra to serve

Salt

Crusty bread or cornbread, to serve

Put the potatoes, onion and garlic in a saucepan and add 1 litre (1¾ pints) of water and a generous pinch of salt. Bring to the boil, then reduce the heat and simmer for 15 minutes or until the potatoes are tender.

Meanwhile, cut out the central ribs from the kale. Stack a few leaves on top of each other and roll them up tightly, then use a sharp knife to cut them into very thin strips, about 3mm (⅛in) wide. Repeat until you have shredded all the kale.

Use a slotted spoon to lift the potatoes out of the liquid and into a bowl, and then mash them with a fork. Return the mash to the pan, add the kale, chorizo and olive oil, then bring back to the boil. You may need to add a little boiling water to just cover the kale. Cook for 4–5 minutes until the kale is just tender.

Taste and adjust the seasoning, then serve immediately, adding a drizzle of olive oil to each bowl, with crusty bread on the side.

Tips

- You need floury/starchy potatoes, which will break down and thicken the soup. Look for Maris Piper or King Edward.
- Omit the chorizo for a vegetarian or vegan version. Instead, you could add extra garlic with the potatoes, a good pinch of smoked paprika when you add the kale, and ground black pepper before serving.

Nettle Soup

Serves **4**
Prep **20 mins**
Cook **30 mins**

V Vegetarian
GF Gluten-free

Free, abundant, easy to identify and rich in vitamin C and iron, nettles have been a welcome springtime food for thousands of years. The oats are a traditional ingredient of nettle soup and add a certain creaminess, but it might still feel a bit worthy, so I'd add some cream for extra richness.

About 200g (7oz), half a carrier bag full, young nettle tops (the first 4 or 6 leaves)

30g (1oz) butter, bacon fat or vegetable oil

2 leeks, chopped

1 potato, about 200g (7oz), diced

4 tbsp porridge oats

1 garlic clove, chopped

1 litre (1¾ pints) vegetable stock

4 tbsp double cream, plus extra to serve

Salt and pepper

Nigella seeds or black and white sesame seeds, to serve (optional)

Wearing rubber gloves, wash the nettles in plenty of salted cold water and then lift them out of the water into a colander. Discard any thick or tough stems (along with any stray twigs). Add the leaves to a pan of boiling water, bring back to the boil for 2 minutes, then drain in a colander and refresh under cold running water. Leave to drain.

Melt the butter in a saucepan over a medium heat, add the leeks, potato and a pinch of salt and cook for about 10 minutes, until softened.

Add the oats, garlic and a pinch of salt and cook for 2–3 minutes. Pour in the stock and bring to the boil, then cover and simmer for about 20 minutes until the potato is soft.

Bring the stock back to the boil, add the nettles and cook, uncovered, for 2–3 minutes.

Blitz the soup with a stick blender until smooth. Taste and adjust the seasoning and stir in the cream. Add a little milk (plant-based if you prefer), stock or just-boiled water if needed to adjust the consistency to your liking.

Serve immediately, with a swirl of cream, and a sprinkling of nigella or sesame seeds, if using.

Tips

• Wearing sturdy gloves and using scissors, snip off the tops of young and tender nettles, between March and May, before the plants have produced flowers.

• Instead of the leeks, use a large onion or 2 bunches of spring onions, including their green tops.

• Replace the garlic with a small handful of wild garlic if it's available, and garnish the soup with wild garlic flowers.

Pea, Lettuce and Mint Soup

Serves   **4**
Prep   **15 mins**
Cook   **15 mins**

(V) Vegan
(GF) Gluten-free

Peas give this soup its bright green colour. It's light and fresh tasting, and packed with vitamins. Serve ungarnished (or with a spoonful of crème fraîche) as a quick, nutritious lunch, or dress it up with mint oil and slices of radish. It's also excellent chilled. A soup for early summer, when peas and the first home-grown lettuces are ready to harvest.

1 tbsp vegetable oil

1 bunch spring onions, chopped

500g (1lb 2oz) frozen peas, or fresh peas (see Tip)

800ml (28fl oz) vegetable stock

150g (5½oz) lettuce, such as cos/romaine, Little Gem or Butterhead, shredded

3 tbsp chopped fresh mint

Salt and pepper

To serve (optional)

Mint oil (page 152)

A few thinly sliced spring onions and/or radishes

Heat the oil in a saucepan over a medium heat, add the spring onions and a pinch of salt and cook for 5–6 minutes until softened.

Add the peas and stir well, then add the stock and bring to the boil. Reduce the heat and simmer for 4–5 minutes.

Add the lettuce and mint, bring back to the boil, then reduce the heat and simmer for 2 minutes.

Blitz the soup with a stick blender until smooth. Taste and adjust the seasoning.

Reheat gently if needed. To serve, drizzle with the mint oil and top with sliced spring onions or radishes, if you like.

Tips

- If you have fresh peas in their pods, weigh them after podding (save the pods to use in your next batch of vegetable stock).
- For a slightly more substantial soup, spoon a small helping of cooked, lightly crushed Jersey Royal potatoes into soup plates, then spoon the soup around.
- You can use the bolted leaves or outside leaves of home-grown lettuces in this soup.
- More or less any lettuce leaves can go into this soup, but avoid red lettuces (which can give a murky colour) and strongly flavoured leaves such as rocket and radicchio (they'll overwhelm the flavours of the peas and mint).

Asparagus Soup

Serves **4**
Prep **20 mins**
Cook **40 mins**

 V Vegetarian
GF Gluten-free

The British asparagus season usually begins in mid-April and traditionally the last spears are cut on 21 June. This silky soup is equally good hot or chilled: it's all about the asparagus. The flavours of Parmesan cheese and cured ham are sublime with asparagus, so you could serve the soup with Parmesan Crisps (page 165) or Prosciutto Crisps (page 164).

700g (1lb 9oz) asparagus

800ml (28fl oz) water or light vegetable stock (see Tip)

30g (1oz) butter

6 shallots (or 2 echalion shallots) or 6 spring onions, chopped

1 potato, cut into small dice

6 tbsp double cream

Salt and pepper

Trim the tips from the asparagus and set aside. Bring the water or stock to the boil in a saucepan. Snap off the woody ends from the asparagus, chop them and add to the boiling water. Reduce the heat and simmer for 15 minutes.

Meanwhile, melt the butter in another saucepan over a medium-low heat, add the shallots and a pinch of salt, and cook for 7–8 minutes until softened. Add the potato, some salt and pepper, and cook for 2–3 minutes.

Strain the hot stock into the saucepan, pressing down on the asparagus ends to extract the maximum flavour. Bring back to the boil, then reduce the heat and simmer for 15 minutes or until the potato is tender.

Roughly chop the asparagus stalks and add them to the pan, bring back to the boil and boil for 3–4 minutes or until just tender. Put the reserved asparagus tips in a colander or steamer basket over the soup and steam for 2–3 minutes or until just tender. Drain and set aside.

Blitz the soup with a stick blender until smooth, then rub it through a fine sieve over a bowl to remove any stringy bits of asparagus. Be sure to scrape the bottom of the sieve to glean all the asparagus. Taste and adjust the seasoning.

Lightly whip 4 tablespoons of the cream to very soft peaks. Stir the remaining cream into the soup and gently reheat until hot. Serve topped with a little cloud of whipped cream and the asparagus tips scattered over.

Tips

- Look out for sprue – thin asparagus stalks that are sometimes sold cheaply – which makes delicious soup.
- The cooking water from boiling potatoes or peas is good instead of stock in this soup.
- If using a vegetable stock cube, be sure to use slightly less than half the amount of stock cube suggested on the pack, or the flavour will overpower the delicate asparagus.
- You can blend and sieve the soup an hour or two in advance (no more, or it may discolour) and keep it in the fridge. Add the cream just before you're ready to reheat and serve.

Spicy New Potato, Coconut and Cashew Soup

Serves **4**
Prep **15 mins**
Cook **30–35 mins**

 Vegan
GF Gluten-free

Spicy flavours are often thought of as warming, but in hot countries such as Thailand, chillies are added to all kinds of food. You can make this vegan meal-in-a-bowl as spicy as you like, depending on how much of the chilli sauce you add.

150g (5½oz) cashew nuts

400g (14oz) new potatoes, scrubbed and cut into 1cm (½in) thick slices

1 tbsp vegetable oil

1 bunch spring onions, sliced

400ml (14fl oz) full-fat coconut milk

1 tbsp sriracha chilli sauce, or to taste

1 tbsp soy sauce, or to taste

Handful of fresh coriander: stalks finely chopped, leaves roughly chopped

100g (3½oz) mangetout, sliced lengthways

Crispy Shallots (page 160), to serve (optional)

Heat a small frying pan over a medium-high heat, add the cashew nuts and dry-fry, stirring often, for about 10 minutes until they begin to turn golden brown. Tip onto a plate and leave to cool. Roughly chop all the cashew nuts; set aside about 50g (1¾oz) to garnish. Put the remaining cashew nuts in a spice grinder, blender or mini chopper, and blitz very briefly to make a rough powder.

Meanwhile, cut the potatoes into spoon-sized pieces if necessary.

Heat the oil in a saucepan over a medium-low heat, add the spring onions and cook for 3–4 minutes until softened.

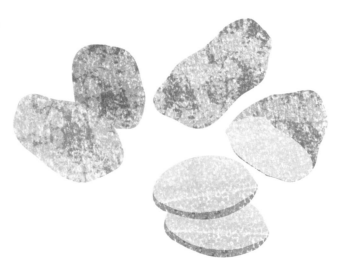

Add the potatoes and stir-fry for 1–2 minutes. Add the ground cashew nuts, coconut milk, sriracha, soy sauce, coriander stalks and 500ml (18fl oz) water. Bring to the boil, then reduce the heat and simmer, uncovered, for 15–20 minutes until the potatoes are tender.

Taste and add more sriracha or soy sauce to get the level of heat and saltiness you like. Add the mangetout and bring back to the boil for 2 minutes.

Ladle into bowls, scatter over the reserved chopped cashew nuts and the coriander leaves, and serve immediately. If you like, add a spoonful of crispy shallots to each bowl.

....

Tip

Sriracha is a hot chilli sauce, originally from Thailand and now popular all around the world. It is a blend of chillies, vinegar, garlic, sugar and salt, used as a condiment for stir-fried dishes, and also with eggs, fried potatoes, chicken, burgers and in wraps and crusty rolls. A bottle will last for months stored in a cool, dark cupboard.

Garden Vegetable Soup

Serves **4**
Prep **15 mins**
Cook **20–25 mins**

 Vegan

GF Gluten-free

Make this your number-one weapon in the fight against food waste. Developed by National Trust chefs to use vegetables and herbs from their kitchen gardens, this classic vegetable soup can be made with whatever's in season. It's also a template for an endlessly adaptable fridge-raid supper. A spring or summer soup might include asparagus, broad beans, green beans or fennel. Later in the year, think about leeks, pumpkins and squashes, cauliflower (include stems and leaves) or parsnips. You can add a big handful of shredded green leaves – such as chard, spinach, spring greens, Savoy cabbage or kale – towards the end of the cooking time: allow 4–5 minutes for simmering.

1 tbsp vegetable oil

1 onion, chopped

2 carrots, diced

1 garlic clove, chopped

200g (7oz) potatoes, diced

About 500g (1lb 2oz) mixed vegetables, such as 170g (6oz) broccoli (including stems), 170g (6oz) fresh podded or frozen peas, 170g (6oz) courgettes, chopped

700ml (1¼ pints) vegetable stock

2 tbsp chopped fresh herbs, such as parsley, chervil or basil, plus extra to serve, or 1 tsp dried mixed herbs

Salt and pepper

Heat the oil in a large saucepan over a medium heat, add all the vegetables and a pinch of salt, and cook for 5–10 minutes until softened.

Add the stock, dried herbs, if using, and a good grinding of pepper, and bring to the boil. Reduce the heat, cover and simmer for 15 minutes or until the vegetables are tender.

Leave to cool slightly, then add the fresh herbs and blitz the soup with a stick blender until smooth. (Alternatively, for a chunkier bowlful, blitz just half the soup.) Taste and adjust the seasoning, and add a little more stock to adjust the consistency to your liking. Serve sprinkled with fresh herbs, if using.

Tips

- If you don't need this to be vegan, use butter instead of vegetable oil for a richer flavour.
- Use your imagination when it comes to garnishing: Parsley and Garlic Butter (page 153); cream, crème fraîche or yogurt; fine ribbon strips of carrot; radishes or cauliflower florets cut into thin slices; croutons, Garlic Breadcrumbs (page 157), toasted seeds or nuts; mascarpone or grated cheese; edible flowers; Basil or Parsley Oil (page 152) or Pesto (page 154).

Spinach Soup with Garlic and Herb Cheese

Serves **4**
Prep **15 mins**
Cook **15 mins**

 Vegetarian

Gluten-free

This vivid green, garlicky soup is quick and easy to make. Spinach grows all year round, but this recipe takes advantage of one of the most useful freezer standbys: frozen spinach.

30g (1oz) butter

1 large onion, chopped

2 plump garlic cloves, chopped

400g (14oz) frozen spinach, defrosted

500ml (18fl oz) vegetable stock

150g (5½oz) full-fat garlic and herb soft cheese

Salt and pepper

To serve

2 tbsp Greek-style yogurt

Freshly snipped chives or chopped fresh parsley

Put a saucepan over a medium heat, add the butter and when it foams add the onion, garlic and a pinch of salt. Cook for 10 minutes or until softened.

Meanwhile, put the spinach in a sieve and press to remove the excess water.

Add the spinach to the pan with the stock and a little salt and pepper, bring to the boil, then reduce the heat and simmer for 5 minutes.

Add the cheese to the hot soup and stir well.

Blitz the soup with a stick blender until smooth. Gently reheat if necessary. Taste and adjust the seasoning. Serve in bowls, topped with a spoonful of yogurt and some snipped chives or chopped parsley.

Tip

To use fresh spinach, you will need about 600g (1lb 5oz) fresh spinach leaves. Wash and pat dry, then add to the softened onion. You will need to add the spinach in batches, stirring until the leaves begin to wilt.

Beetroot and Horseradish Soup

Serves **4**
Prep **20 mins**
Cook **about 1 hour**

VØ Vegan
GF Gluten-free

The rich colour of this soup makes you feel warm just by looking at it, and horseradish adds a peppery touch that perfectly complements the beetroot's sweet earthiness. This is always a popular choice when it's on the menu at National Trust cafés.

1 tbsp vegetable oil

1 onion, chopped

2 carrots, chopped

2 celery sticks, chopped

2 garlic cloves, chopped

1 tbsp tomato purée

500g (1lb 2oz) raw beetroot, trimmed, scrubbed and diced

850ml (1½ pints) vegetable stock, plus extra if needed

2 bay leaves

1 tbsp cider vinegar, or white or red wine vinegar

20g (¾oz) fresh horseradish, peeled and grated (see Tip)

Salt and pepper

To serve

100ml (3½fl oz) soured cream, double cream, crème fraîche, or plant-based alternative

Chopped fresh dill or snipped chives

Heat the oil in a saucepan over a medium heat, add the onion and cook for 5 minutes. Stir in the carrots, celery, garlic, tomato purée and some salt and pepper, cover the pan and cook for a further 10 minutes.

Add the beetroot, stock, bay leaves and another pinch of salt. Bring to the boil, then reduce the heat, cover and simmer for 30–40 minutes until the beetroot is tender.

Leave the soup to cool slightly, then remove the bay leaves. Blitz the soup thoroughly using a stick blender, then add the vinegar, horseradish and salt and pepper to taste, and blend again. If the soup seems thick, add a little extra stock or boiling water.

Reheat if necessary, then serve topped with your chosen cream and a sprinkling of fresh dill or chives.

Tips

- Don't be tempted to use vacuum packs of ready-cooked beetroot, as it doesn't have the same depth of flavour.
- Keep fresh horseradish in a paper bag in the fridge or cut it into small pieces and freeze. Do not peel until you are ready to use it. Beware that when you peel and grate it, fresh horseradish releases pungent compounds that can make your eyes water.
- If fresh horseradish is unavailable, replace with a teaspoonful or two of hot horseradish sauce, to taste.

Tomato and Fennel Soup

Serves **4–6**
Prep **15 mins**
Cook **30 mins**

V0 Vegan
GF Gluten-free

Tomato, fennel and lemon are the best of friends in this simple soup, which highlights the fennel's subtle aniseed flavour. It's inspired by a recipe developed by the National Trust chefs. Home-grown tomatoes and fennel are at their best from July to September.

1 tbsp olive oil

3 echalion shallots, chopped

1 tsp fennel seeds, crushed

1 large carrot, diced

1 medium–large fennel bulb, about 300g (10½oz), thinly sliced, feathery fronds reserved

½ lemon: rind pared off in strips, juice squeezed

700ml (1¼ pints) vegetable stock

400g ripe tomatoes, skinned, deseeded and chopped (see Tip, page 79)

Extra virgin olive oil, to serve

Salt and pepper

Heat the oil in a saucepan over a medium heat, add the shallots and a pinch of salt and cook for 6–8 minutes until beginning to soften. Add the fennel seeds, carrot, most of the fennel (reserving a little to garnish) and three or four strips of lemon rind. Cook for a further 6–8 minutes, stirring from time to time, until the vegetables are aromatic.

Add the stock and a little salt and pepper, and bring to the boil. Reduce the heat, partly cover the pan and simmer for 15–20 minutes until the vegetables are tender.

Remove the lemon rind, add the tomatoes and bring to the boil. Reduce the heat and simmer for 5 minutes. Add 1 teaspoon of lemon juice and blitz the soup with a stick blender until smooth. Taste and adjust the seasoning, adding a little more lemon juice if needed. Reheat if needed.

Serve in bowls. Scatter over the reserved thinly sliced fennel and fennel fronds, adding a drizzle of extra virgin olive oil and a few shreds of lemon zest if you like.

Tips

- If your tomatoes are not ripe and full of flavour, add 1 tablespoon of tomato purée along with the fennel seeds and carrot.

- Instead of fresh tomatoes, you could use a 400g tin of chopped tomatoes.

Tomato, Red Onion and Oregano Soup

Serves **4**
Prep **15 mins**
Cook **40–50 mins**

 Vegan

The flavour of roasted tomatoes shines through this simple soup, with subtle background notes from roasted red onions, garlic and oregano – a lovely way to use the last of the summer's tomatoes.

1kg (2lb 3oz) ripe tomatoes, halved

3 red onions, cut into wedges

2 plump garlic cloves, in their skins

4 oregano sprigs, plus about 10 leaves, or 1½ tsp dried oregano

2 tbsp olive oil

700ml (1¼ pints) vegetable stock

1–2 tsp balsamic vinegar, to taste

Pinch of sugar, or to taste

Salt and pepper

Garlic Breadcrumbs (page 157), to serve

Preheat the oven to 220°C/200°C fan/gas 7 and line a roasting tin with baking paper or foil. If the tomatoes have hard, woody centres, cut these out with a small sharp knife. Put the tomatoes (cut-side down) and the onion wedges in the prepared roasting tin, then add the garlic and oregano sprigs or dried oregano. Drizzle with the olive oil and season with salt and pepper.

Roast for 20–25 minutes, but check the garlic after 15 minutes: it should feel soft but you don't want it to burn. If necessary, remove the garlic and continue to roast the onions and tomatoes until lightly charred at the edges.

Leave to cool slightly, then pinch off and discard the tomato and garlic skins (there's no need to pick off every last bit of tomato skin). Discard any tough bits of oregano stalk.

Lift up the baking paper or foil by the corners and carefully tip the contents into a large saucepan. Add the stock, 1 teaspoon of the balsamic vinegar and a pinch of sugar. Bring to the boil, then reduce the heat and simmer for 5 minutes.

Add the fresh oregano leaves, if using, and blitz the soup with a stick blender until smooth. Taste and adjust the seasoning, adding more balsamic vinegar or sugar to taste. Reheat gently and serve with garlic breadcrumbs.

Smoky Sweetcorn Soup

Serves **4**
Prep **15 mins**
Cook **25–30 mins**

 Vegan
Gluten-free

Chipotle paste gives this velvety soup a subtle smokiness to lift the sweetness of the corn. Frozen sweetcorn is available all year round; it's frozen at peak condition to capture its flavour and nutritional content. This soup is inspired by a recipe developed by the National Trust chefs.

1 tbsp vegetable oil

1 large onion, finely chopped

1 garlic clove, chopped

1 potato, chopped

1 tsp fresh thyme leaves, or ½ tsp dried thyme

1½ tsp chipotle chilli paste (see Tip)

500g (1lb 2oz) frozen sweetcorn

850ml (1½ pints) vegetable stock, plus extra if needed

Salt and pepper

Chilli oil

2 tbsp cold-pressed rapeseed oil or extra virgin olive oil

¼–½ fresh red chilli, to taste, deseeded and very finely chopped

Heat the oil in a saucepan over a medium heat, add the onion and a pinch of salt, and cook for 8–10 minutes until softened.

Add the garlic, potato, thyme and chipotle paste and continue to cook, stirring, for 3 minutes.

Add the corn, pour in the stock and bring to the boil, then reduce the heat and simmer for 15 minutes or until the potato is tender.

Meanwhile, make the chilli oil: heat the oil in a small pan, add the chilli, and as soon as it begins to sizzle, remove from the heat.

Blitz the soup with a stick blender until smooth, then rub it through a fine sieve to remove the fibrous bits of sweetcorn and obtain a really velvety soup. Taste and adjust the seasoning, and add a little more stock or just-boiled water to adjust the consistency to your liking. Reheat gently. Serve drizzled with the chilli oil.

Tips

- Chipotle paste can be fierce: the label may give a clue as to whether it is hot, or very hot. I've used only a small amount so as not to overpower the sweetcorn, but if you love your chillies add a little more.

- If you can't get chipotle chilli paste you could substitute a pinch of dried chilli flakes and a pinch of smoked paprika.

- For a more substantial and filling soup, when reheating, add some tinned red kidney beans or pinto beans (drained and rinsed), or any beans you have cooked from dried.

- Use leftover chipotle chilli paste to add a rich, smoky flavour to pork, chicken, and bean dishes, from chilli con carne to baked beans – or stir a spoonful into Black Bean Soup (page 66).

Roasted Cauliflower and Almond Soup

Serves **4–6**
Prep **20 mins**
Cook **25–30 mins**

 Vegan
GF Gluten-free

Cumin brings warm, earthy depth to this creamy soup. Toasted almonds add a delicious nutty flavour and crunchy texture, along with crispy roasted cauliflower leaves.

1 cauliflower

1 large onion, roughly chopped

3 large garlic cloves, peeled

3 tbsp olive oil

4 tsp ground cumin

4 tbsp flaked almonds, to taste

500ml (18fl oz) unsweetened plant-based milk, plus extra if needed

1 bay leaf

2 thyme sprigs

½ tsp ground turmeric

500ml (18fl oz) vegetable stock, plus extra if needed

Salt and pepper

Tips

- You could use dairy milk if you're not vegan.
- A spoonful of cold Greek-style yogurt on top would bring another dimension of creamy flavour.

Preheat the oven to 200°C/180°C fan/gas 6. Remove the leaves from the cauliflower and set aside. Cut the cauliflower into equal-sized florets and use as much of the stem as you can, cutting it into small chunks.

Put in a large roasting tin, add the onion and garlic and drizzle over 2 tablespoons of the oil, 3 teaspoons of the cumin, and a good pinch of salt and some pepper. Stir to mix well. Roast for 20 minutes or until softening and lightly charred, turning halfway through.

Once the cauliflower is in the oven, quickly sort through the leaves to pick out the smaller, tender ones. Strip the leafy parts from the larger, thicker stems. Put all the leaves in a small baking tin, add the remaining olive oil and cumin and a little salt, and cook in the oven for 10–15 minutes until crisp and charred in places. Tip onto a plate and set aside.

Spread the flaked almonds on a small baking sheet and toast in the oven for 1 minute or until golden but not brown. Tip onto a plate and set aside.

While the cauliflower is roasting, pour the milk into a saucepan, add the bay leaf, thyme and turmeric, and put over a low heat to bring the milk up to simmering point. Remove from the heat, cover and leave to infuse for 10–20 minutes.

Using a slotted spoon, fish the bay leaf and thyme out of the milk. Add the roasted cauliflower, onion and garlic to the milk, then add the stock. Bring to the boil, then reduce the heat and simmer for 5 minutes or until the cauliflower is soft.

Blitz the soup with a stick blender until smooth. Taste and adjust the seasoning, and add a little extra stock or milk to adjust the consistency to your liking. Reheat if needed and serve topped with the roasted cauliflower leaves and toasted flaked almonds.

Corn Chowder

Serves **4**
Prep **20 mins**
Cook **50–60 mins**

V Vegetarian

GF Gluten-free

In late summer, look out for fresh corn on the cob, still encased in its green leaves. This recipe gets maximum flavour from the cobs – once stripped of their kernels – by simmering them in the stock, but this hearty soup is cosy and comforting at any time of the year if made with tinned or frozen sweetcorn.

4 fresh corn cobs, leaves removed

600ml (1 pint) vegetable stock

4 tsp vegetable oil

20g (¾oz) butter

1 onion, finely chopped

2 celery sticks, finely chopped

1 large garlic clove, finely chopped

1 bay leaf

300g (10½oz) potatoes, diced

300ml (10½fl oz) full-fat milk

½ bunch spring onions, sliced

Salt and pepper

Stand each corn cob on end on a chopping board. Use a sharp knife to slice down and cut off the kernels. Run the back of your knife down the sides of the cobs to collect the remnants of the kernels. Set aside a small handful of the kernels to garnish.

Put the stock in a large saucepan and bring to the boil. Add the stripped corn cobs, then reduce the heat and simmer for 30 minutes while you prepare the remaining vegetables. Strain the stock and set aside.

Heat 3 teaspoons of the vegetable oil with the butter in a large saucepan over a medium heat, add the onion, celery, garlic and a pinch of salt, and cook for 7–8 minutes until softened.

Add the stock, bay leaf and potatoes and bring to the boil. Add the corn, then reduce the heat, cover and simmer for 10–15 minutes until the potatoes are almost tender. Add the milk and simmer very gently for a further 5–10 minutes until the potatoes are soft.

Using a slotted spoon, remove about half the vegetables and set aside. Discard the bay leaf. Blitz the soup with a stick blender until smooth, then return the unblended vegetables to the pan. Taste and adjust the seasoning. Reheat if needed.

Heat the remaining 1 teaspoon oil in a small saucepan over a medium-high heat, add the reserved sweetcorn and stir-fry for 2–3 minutes. Add the spring onions, stir-fry briefly, then season with a pinch of salt. Spoon over the soup and serve immediately, finishing with a grinding of black pepper.

Tips

- You can make the soup up to 2 days in advance and keep it covered in the fridge; reheat gently until piping hot. (Note: this soup doesn't freeze well due to the combination of potatoes and milk.)
- For vegans, replace the butter and milk with vegetable oil and unsweetened plant-based milk.
- If you're not vegetarian, you might like to begin by frying 4 rashers of bacon until crisp. Remove and set aside, then cook the onion in the same pan. Crumble the bacon and scatter over the soup just before serving.
- If you can't get fresh corn cobs, you will need about 300g (10½oz) frozen sweetcorn or 2 x 200g (7oz) tins sweetcorn, drained and rinsed.

Thai-Style Spiced Squash Soup

Serves **4**
Prep **20 mins**
Cook **30–40 mins**

Vegan
Gluten-free

This wonderfully warming soup is easy to make and is a popular seasonal treat in the cafés at many National Trust places – especially those that grow their own squashes and pumpkins. Thai curry pastes vary in spiciness, so unless you're making this for chilli-heat fiends, use the smaller amount of paste: you can always add more chilli on top.

1 tbsp vegetable oil

1 onion or 5 shallots, finely chopped

1–2 tbsp Thai red curry paste, to taste

1 small squash, about 1kg (2lb 3oz), halved, deseeded, peeled and cut into small chunks (you need about 750g/1lb 10oz prepared squash)

700ml (1¼ pints) vegetable stock or water

200ml (7fl oz) full-fat coconut milk

1 tsp soft brown sugar

Soy sauce, to taste

Juice of ½–1 lime, to taste

Salt and pepper

To serve

1–2 fresh red chillies, deseeded and thinly sliced

Handful of fresh coriander leaves

Crispy Shallots (page 160)

Heat the oil in a saucepan over a medium heat, add the onion or shallots and cook for 5 minutes.

Add the Thai curry paste and cook for 2 minutes. Add the squash and stir to coat.

Add the stock and coconut milk, and bring to the boil, then reduce the heat and simmer, uncovered, for 20–30 minutes until the squash is tender.

Blitz the soup with a stick blender until smooth. Taste and adjust the seasoning, adding sugar, soy sauce and lime juice to balance the flavours. Reheat if needed. Serve topped with sliced red chilli, fresh coriander and some crispy shallots.

Tips

• Use any variety of squash or pumpkin, but remember that they vary in flavour, so be sure to taste and adjust the seasonings as needed. You need only a small squash – preferably less than 1kg (2lb 3oz) – but if you have a larger one, leftovers will keep in the fridge for a few days: cut into chunks and roast or add to stews.

• Not all Thai red curry paste is vegan, so check the label when you shop.

• You can freeze this soup, but reheat it very gently, stirring frequently, to prevent the coconut milk from separating.

• Don't waste the squash seeds: you can toast them to make a healthy snack or a topping for soups and salads (page 158).

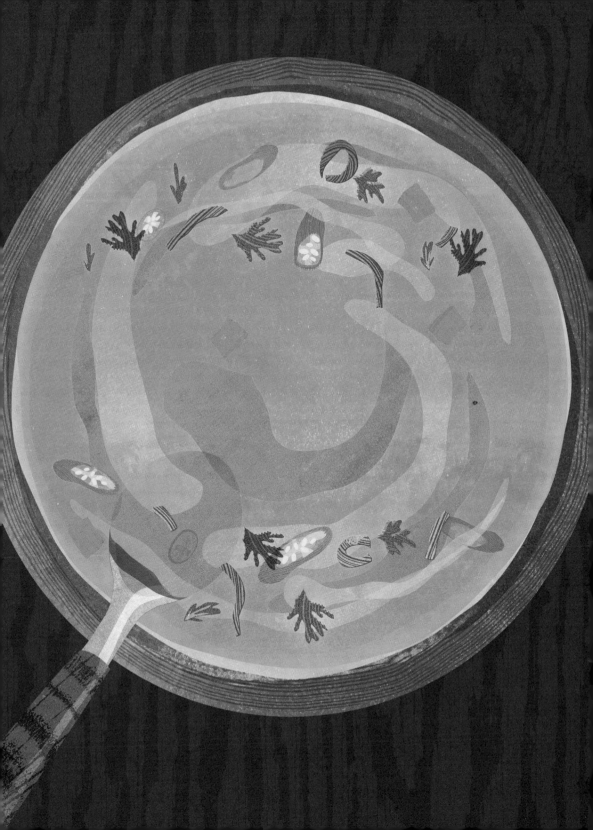

Squash and Red Pepper Soup with Leek and Lime

Serves **4**
Prep **35 mins**
Cook **1 hour**

 Vegan
GF Gluten-free

A soup for autumn, when pumpkins and squash are in season. Roasting the squash and red pepper intensifies their flavours, while lime and chilli lift the natural sweetness of the vegetables. This recipe includes a zingy topping that combines the toasted squash seeds with herbs and lime.

½ small squash, deseeded (reserve the seeds) and cut into 2–3cm (1–1¼in) chunks (you need about 500g/1lb 2oz prepared squash)

2 red peppers, halved and deseeded

3 tbsp olive oil, plus about 3 tbsp for the topping

2 leeks, thinly sliced

1 small fresh red chilli, deseeded and chopped

2 garlic cloves, chopped, plus 1 small garlic clove, very finely chopped

850ml (1½ pints) vegetable stock, plus extra if needed

Grated zest and juice of 1 lime

Handful of flat-leaf parsley, chopped

Handful of fresh coriander, chopped

Salt and pepper

Preheat the oven to 200°C/180°C fan/gas 6. Cut the skin off the squash if necessary, though there's no need to peel thin-skinned squash, such as butternut. Put the squash and peppers in a large roasting tin and toss with 1½ tablespoons of the olive oil and some salt and pepper, then turn the peppers skin-side up. Roast for 30 minutes or until tender and lightly charred.

Move the peppers together in the tin and cover with an upturned bowl. Leave for 15 minutes to help loosen the skins. Peel off the skins.

While the squash is roasting, wash the squash seeds, rubbing off the pulp, then dry thoroughly on a clean tea towel.

Heat ½ tablespoon of the oil in a small frying pan over a medium-high heat, add the seeds and stir for 3–4 minutes until beginning to turn golden. Drain on kitchen paper and leave to cool.

Heat 1 tablespoon of the oil in a large saucepan over a medium-low heat. Add the leeks and a pinch of salt and cook for 10–15 minutes until soft. Add the chilli and the 2 chopped garlic cloves and cook for 2 minutes.

Add the roasted squash and skinned peppers to the pan, then add the stock and bring to the boil. Reduce the heat, cover and simmer for 10 minutes.

To make the topping, put a handful of the toasted squash seeds in a small blender or mini chopper, add the lime zest and a good squeeze of juice, the parsley, coriander, finely chopped garlic and some salt and pepper. Blitz briefly to roughly chop the seeds and make a coarse paste. Stir in 3 tablespoons of olive oil, then taste and add more lime juice, salt, pepper or olive oil if you like.

Blitz the soup with a stick blender until smooth. Taste and adjust the seasoning, adding at least half the lime juice or more if you like. Add a little more stock or just-boiled water to adjust the consistency to your liking. Reheat if needed. Serve in bowls and spoon over a little of the seed and herb oil topping.

Tips

- Use any variety of squash or pumpkin, but remember that they vary in flavour – and larger pumpkins may be watery and need longer roasting. Be sure to taste and adjust the seasonings.
- For an everyday soup, you could replace the topping with the simply roasted squash seeds, seasoned with a little sea salt, or shop-bought toasted pumpkin seeds, or shop-bought or homemade Dukkah (page 159). Serve with wedges of fresh lime to squeeze over the soup.
- Leftover squash will keep in the fridge for a few days. To use it, cut into chunks and add to stews, or roast as a side dish.

Cauliflower Cheese Soup

Serves **4**
Prep **15 mins**
Cook **40 mins**

V — Vegetarian
GF — Gluten-free

Cauliflower cheese is high on the comfort food charts – it's the inspiration for this soothing soup. The new crop of cauliflowers appears in the autumn, with a long season that extends through to spring.

1 small cauliflower

40g (1½oz) butter

1 large leek (white part only), thinly sliced

400ml (14fl oz) vegetable stock

400ml (14fl oz) whole milk

1 bay leaf

Piece of rind from a hard cheese such as Parmesan, pecorino or a vegetarian alternative (optional)

4 tbsp single or double cream

120–150g (4¼–5½oz) mature Cheddar, to taste, grated

1–1½ tsp mustard, to taste

Salt and pepper

To serve

Good pinch of cayenne pepper

Snipped chives (optional)

Cut the cauliflower into small florets and cut the stem into thin slices.

Melt the butter in a large saucepan over a medium-low heat, add the leek and a pinch of salt, and cook for 8–10 minutes until softened.

Add the cauliflower and another pinch of salt to the softened leek, and stir well. Cover with a butter wrapper or a disc of baking paper, turn the heat to low, then put the lid on the pan and cook for 15 minutes or until the cauliflower has softened, stirring halfway through.

Add the stock, milk and bay leaf, and bring to the boil. Reduce the heat, add the cheese rind, if using, then cover and simmer for 10 minutes or until the cauliflower is tender.

Leave to cool slightly, then use a slotted spoon to lift out the cheese rind and bay leaf. Add the cream, 120g (4¼oz) of the cheese and 1 teaspoon of the mustard, and blitz the soup with a stick blender until smooth. Taste and adjust the seasoning and flavour: you might also want to add more cheese or mustard.

Reheat gently, if needed, and serve with a sprinkling of cayenne pepper and chives, if you like.

Tips

- Use any mustard you like: French or English, smooth or wholegrain.
- Cooking the cauliflower under paper helps it to cook in its own steam without burning.
- Prepare ahead up to the point where the cauliflower has been simmered until tender. Reheat gently, then blend with the cream, cheese and mustard; do not allow to boil after adding the cheese.

Caramelised Onion and Cider Soup with Cheese Toasts

Serves **4**
Prep **20 mins**
Cook **1 hour**

V Vegetarian

Make a meal of ever-popular onion soup by serving it with a pile of crisp cheese toasts.

1 tbsp vegetable oil

40g (1½oz) butter

1kg (2lb 3oz) onions, thinly sliced

2 garlic cloves, chopped

2 tsp fresh thyme leaves, or ½ tsp dried thyme

2 tbsp plain flour

250ml (9fl oz) dry cider

850ml (1½ pints) vegetable stock (see Tip)

Salt and pepper

Cheese toasts

12 small slices sourdough or French bread

150g (5½oz) Gruyère or mature Cheddar, grated

Heat the oil and butter in a large, heavy-based saucepan over a medium heat, add the onions and some salt and pepper, and stir well. Turn the heat to low and cook for 25 minutes, stirring from time to time. Turn the heat to medium-high and cook for 10 minutes or until the onions are soft, dark brown and caramelised, but not burnt.

Add the garlic and thyme and cook for 30 seconds, then stir in the flour and cook for 1 minute, stirring all the time. Stir in the cider and cook until the mixture thickens. Gradually stir in the stock, bring to the boil, then reduce the heat, partly cover the pan and leave to simmer for 20 minutes.

Meanwhile, make the cheese toasts. Toast the bread lightly on both sides. Top with the cheese and grill until the cheese begins to bubble and brown in patches.

Taste the soup and adjust the seasoning. Serve in bowls. Add a cheese toast to each bowl and serve the remaining toasts on the side.

Tips

- This is traditionally made with beef or veal stock, but you can use a good chicken or vegetable stock. Add 1 teaspoon of Marmite with the stock, if you like.
- There are many variations on this traditional French soup, some of which require sturdy heatproof or flameproof bowls, which are popped into the oven or under the grill to melt the cheese. Some recipes place a layer of bread in the bowl before adding the soup, and then more bread and cheese on top.

Sweet Potato, Tomato and Ginger Soup

Serves **4**
Prep **20 mins**
Cook **35–40 mins**

 Vegan
GF Gluten-free

Sweet potatoes were enjoyed in Elizabethan England before today's common potato was grown here; the two are not related. In this spicy, warming soup their nutty sweetness is offset by a touch of tomato and ginger. A spoonful of coconut coriander chutney makes a lively addition to the soup, but if you don't have time, a simple garnish of coconut flakes, coconut milk or yogurt and coriander leaves would look good. Serve with a pile of poppadoms.

1 tbsp vegetable oil

1 large onion, chopped

2 garlic cloves, chopped

1cm (½in) fresh ginger, peeled and grated

Pinch of dried chilli flakes

700g (1lb 9oz) sweet potatoes, peeled and chopped into 2cm (¾in) pieces

200g (7oz) tinned chopped tomatoes or passata

700ml (1¼ pints) vegetable stock

2 tsp garam masala

200ml (7fl oz) full-fat coconut milk

Fresh coriander leaves, to garnish

Salt

Coconut coriander chutney

50g (1¾oz) grated fresh or frozen coconut, or 30g (1oz) desiccated coconut

3 tbsp coconut milk, plus extra if needed

1 small green chilli, deseeded and finely chopped

3 tbsp finely chopped fresh coriander

2 tbsp finely chopped fresh mint leaves

Pinch of sugar

Pinch of salt

Juice of 1 lime

Heat the oil in a large saucepan over a medium heat, add the onion, garlic, ginger, chilli and a pinch of salt, and cook for 7–8 minutes until beginning to soften.

Add the sweet potatoes and cook, stirring, for 3 minutes. Add the tomatoes or passata and stock, and bring to the boil. Reduce the heat, cover and simmer for 20–25 minutes until the potatoes are tender.

To make the coconut chutney, if using desiccated coconut, put it in a bowl and cover with just-boiled water. Leave to soak for 20 minutes, then strain through a sieve, pressing to remove the liquid. Mix the coconut with the coconut milk, chilli, herbs, sugar and salt, adding lime juice for sharpness and a little more coconut milk if necessary to make a thick paste. Transfer to a small serving bowl.

Add the garam masala to the soup along with most of the coconut milk (reserving a little to garnish, if you like). Remove about two-thirds of the soup and blitz with a stick blender until smooth, then return it to the pan. Taste and adjust the seasoning. Reheat gently if needed. Serve the soup with the coconut chutney alongside.

Celeriac Soup with Toasted Hazelnuts

Serves **4**
Prep **20 mins**
Cook **55 mins**

 Vegan

Gluten-free

This is inspired by a recipe created by National Trust chefs for a winter café menu. If you're lucky enough to gather a good harvest of hazelnuts, save some for this soup. Use either skinned or blanched hazelnuts: the skins will loosen when you toast the nuts. Look out for celeriac when it's in season from October through to March.

40g (1½oz) hazelnuts

1 tbsp vegetable oil

1 large onion, chopped

1 large garlic clove, chopped

1 small celeriac, cut into 2cm (¾in) chunks

1 potato, chopped

700ml (1¼ pints) vegetable stock, plus extra if needed

200ml (7fl oz) unsweetened hazelnut milk

Sea salt flakes

Ground white or black pepper

To serve

2 tbsp roughly torn flat-leaf parsley

Dried cranberries, roughly chopped (optional)

Heat a small frying pan over a medium-high heat, add the hazelnuts and dry-fry, stirring often, for 10–15 minutes until they begin to smell toasty – they should be well toasted but not burnt. (Alternatively, if your oven is already on, at 190°C/170°C fan/gas 5, for another dish, spread the hazelnuts on a baking tray and put in the oven for 5–10 minutes. Shake them occasionally and watch them closely so that they don't burn.)

Tip the nuts onto a clean tea towel and rub off the skins. Put onto a chopping board and add a good pinch of sea salt flakes, then leave to cool. Use a rolling pin to break up the hazelnuts and set aside.

Heat the oil in a saucepan over a medium-low heat, add the onion and a pinch of salt, and cook for 8–10 minutes until softened and pale golden.

Add the garlic and stir for 30 seconds, then add the celeriac, potato and another pinch of salt, and stir well. Add the stock and bring to the boil, then reduce the heat, partly cover and simmer for 20–30 minutes until the vegetables are soft.

Add the hazelnut milk and blitz the soup with a stick blender until smooth. Taste and adjust the seasoning, and add a little more stock or water to adjust the consistency to your liking.

Mix the salted toasted hazelnuts with the flat-leaf parsley. Gently reheat the soup and serve topped with the hazelnuts and parsley. If you like, add some cranberries.

Tips

- If you can't eat nuts, leave out the hazelnuts and use soya milk instead of hazelnut milk. You could top the soup with shop-bought beetroot crisps for colour and crunch.

Foraging

Spending time in nature has been shown to improve wellbeing by reducing stress and boosting the immune system, and there is no better way to connect with nature through all your senses than by foraging for wild food.

The first rule of foraging is to check the ID of any plant, to be 100 per cent certain that it's edible *before* you pick it. Ideally check two or three sources, as a single image might not be representative of the specimen in front of you. Only pick what's plentiful, that you know you'll use, and always leave some to maintain the habitat. Pick away from paths and roads to avoid dust and pollution, and don't pick too low down, as dogs, foxes and other animals may have left their mark.

You'll need: clothes that protect your arms and legs from scratches; a pair of scissors; protective gloves if you're gathering nettles; bags, baskets and containers with lids if you're gathering berries. You can also collect fungi, but it is essential to learn how to do so while accompanied by an experienced fungi gatherer, as some poisonous species appear similar to common mushrooms.

When trying a new species, eat only a little at first, in case it doesn't agree with you. Most fungi are best cooked. Rinse leaves, berries and sturdier flowers in a bowl of cold water (I add salt to draw out any bugs). If using them for a garnish, pat them dry. Rather than washing delicate flowers, gently shake them over a sheet of paper to dislodge insects.

Leaves should be eaten while they are young and tender – certainly before the plant flowers, as the leaves become increasingly bitter as they get older.

Nettles and wild garlic are plentiful and fairly easy to identify; wild garlic also produces edible white flowers. Both make delicious soup. Other edible leaves that have a garlicky smell when crushed are garlic mustard and three-cornered leek; they can be added to soups at the end of cooking time, chopped as garnishes, or used in pesto.

Fresh young hawthorn leaves can be chopped and used in place of parsley to scatter over soups. The leaves of sorrel, another plant that's common throughout the British Isles, have a distinctively sour and lemony taste, and in France they are used to make soups and sauces – try it in the wild garlic variation of Watercress Soup (page 18).

Flowers make simple yet striking garnishes. Gorse can flower at any time of the year and its open petals make a bright yellow garnish – but beware of the sharp spines. Dandelion petals are less hazardous and super-easy to find; they'll need a good wash, then snip off and discard the green parts of the flowers. The beautiful star-shaped blue flowers of borage and the purple flower heads of red clover are also easy to find throughout the summer – separate the florets.

Berries, with the exception of blackberries, are seldom found in large quantities, but, if you're lucky enough to find wild strawberries, raspberries, gooseberries or bilberries, it will make your summer foraging walk truly memorable – and you could use them in Red Fruit Soup (page 143).

Nuts offer ideal foraging for soup lovers. Easy to recognise, they store well and are perfect toasted and lightly crushed as a garnish. Hazelnuts generally ripen and fall from their trees in September. Nuts already on the ground may be empty shells that the tree shed before the nuts developed, so check a few before you gather them. In October and November look for sweet chestnuts and walnuts – some years will produce a better harvest than others. Step on the prickly cases of sweet chestnuts and twist your foot to prise out the glossy nuts. Walnut juice will stain everything brown, so use old gloves to separate the nuts from their green husks. Chestnuts need to be cooked (boiled or roasted, see page 51) and peeled before you eat them.

Wild mushrooms are delicious as an ingredient or garnish, but, as mentioned above, it's vital to identify correctly before you pick. It's worth taking time to learn more about edible fungi: an autumn forage can bring rich rewards.

The National Trust supports responsible foraging on many of its properties. For more information, see **nationaltrust.org.uk/who-we-are/about-us/our-policy-on-foraging-for-wild-food**

Learn more about foraging, identifying and using wild plants at **wildfooduk.com** and **britishlocalfood.com**

Notes While the publishers and I have taken every care in the preparation of this book, neither I, the National Trust nor HarperCollins can accept any responsibility or liability for the end results of the recipes featured. Always check several sources to ensure that you have identified correctly, as some wild plants have dangerous lookalikes. Avoid any unfamiliar ingredients if you have any allergies, medical conditions or you are pregnant or breastfeeding.

There is a general right to collect fruit, flowers, foliage and fungi provided that they are growing wild and that you are picking for personal use; however, it is illegal to dig up roots without the landowner's permission. Land designated under the Countryside and Rights of Way Act does not necessarily include the right to forage. It's technically illegal to remove plants from a Site of Special Scientific Interest (SSSI).

Serves **4**
Prep **20 mins**
Cook **35 mins**

V Vegan
GF Gluten-free

Chestnut and Mushroom Soup with Orange Gremolata

Gremolata – a vibrant mix of citrus zest, garlic and parsley – adds a pop of colour and freshness to this satisfying, nutty soup. Use ready-roasted unsweetened chestnuts (from a pack or bought freshly cooked from a street seller and peeled while hot – if you can resist eating them), or chestnuts that you've gathered yourself.

1 tbsp olive oil

1 onion, finely chopped

1 large carrot, diced

1 celery stick, finely chopped

2 tsp finely chopped fresh rosemary

2 garlic cloves, very finely chopped

250g (9oz) mushrooms, roughly chopped

200g (7oz) roasted chestnuts, roughly chopped (see Tip)

600ml (1 pint) vegetable stock

2 bay leaves

Grated zest and juice of 1 orange

2 tbsp finely chopped flat-leaf parsley

Salt and pepper

Heat the oil in a saucepan over a medium-low heat, add the onion, carrot, celery and some salt and pepper, and cook for 15 minutes or until softened.

Add 1 teaspoon of the rosemary and two-thirds of the garlic to the pan and cook for 1 minute, then add the mushrooms, turn up the heat and cook for 3–4 minutes, stirring once or twice, until golden.

Add the chestnuts, stock, bay leaves, 4–5 tablespoons of the orange juice, to taste, and a little more salt. Bring to the boil, then reduce the heat, cover and simmer for 10–15 minutes until the vegetables are tender.

To make the orange gremolata, mix the orange zest, parsley and the remaining garlic in a small bowl.

Leave the soup to cool slightly, remove the bay leaves, then taste and adjust the seasoning, adding a little more rosemary and orange juice if you like. Remove a third of the soup and set aside. Blitz the soup with a stick blender until smooth, then return the unblended soup to the pan. Gently reheat if needed and serve with the gremolata to sprinkle over.

Tips

- To roast fresh chestnuts (having carefully removed the prickly cases), cut a long slit through the shell of each nut (this stops them from exploding), discarding any that are soft or have holes in them. Spread on a baking sheet and roast at 200°C/180°C fan/gas 6 for 20 minutes or until the slits have widened, exposing the nuts. Cover with a clean tea towel and leave for a few minutes until they're just cool enough to handle, then peel off the shells and inner skins.

- A weight of 350g (12oz) whole chestnuts should yield about 200g (7oz) peeled.

- If you're not vegetarian, you could fry 100g (3½oz) of pancetta, lardons or chopped bacon before adding the onion, carrot and celery; use chicken stock instead of vegetable stock; if you have a piece of Parmesan rind, add it with the stock, removing it before you blend the soup.

Creamy Mushroom Soup

Serves **4**
Prep **15 mins, plus soaking**
Cook **35 mins**

V Vegetarian
GF Gluten-free

Rich with mushroom flavour, this soup is a perfect choice for autumn days and is always a favourite in the National Trust cafés. Serve it in a mug, or add an extra layer of flavour and texture with garlic breadcrumbs or croutons.

20g (¾oz) dried mushrooms

200ml (7fl oz) boiling water

30g (1oz) butter

1 onion, or 2 echalion shallots or 8 small round shallots, chopped

2 large garlic cloves, chopped

2 tbsp fresh thyme leaves

600g (1lb 5oz) fresh mushrooms, sliced

500ml (18fl oz) vegetable stock

85ml (3fl oz) milk

4 tbsp double cream

Garlic Breadcrumbs (page 157) or Croutons (page 156), to serve (optional)

Salt and pepper

Put the dried mushrooms in a small bowl or jug and pour over the boiling water. Leave to soak for at least 1 hour (you can soak them overnight if you wish).

Put a saucepan over a medium-high heat and add the butter. When it foams, add the onion, garlic, thyme and a pinch of salt. Turn the heat to low and cook for 7–10 minutes until softened, stirring occasionally.

Turn up the heat, add the sliced fresh mushrooms and cook for 3–4 minutes, stirring once or twice, until golden. (If you like, you can remove a couple of tablespoons of the cooked mushrooms and set aside to garnish.)

Reduce the heat, cover and continue to cook for 8–10 minutes, stirring occasionally to prevent sticking, until the mushrooms have softened and released some of their liquid.

Using a slotted spoon, lift the soaked dried mushrooms out of their liquid and add to the pan. Carefully pour in most of the soaking liquid, leaving the gritty bits behind.

Pour in the stock and milk, and season with salt and pepper. Bring to the boil, then reduce the heat, cover and simmer for 8–10 minutes.

Leave to cool slightly, then add the cream and blitz the soup with a stick blender until smooth. Taste and adjust the seasoning. Reheat if needed. Serve in mugs or bowls, topped with the reserved mushrooms and garlic breadcrumbs or croutons, if you like.

Tip

If you have foraged some wild mushrooms, you can use them instead of some of the regular mushrooms, or fry them in butter over a high heat and add them as a garnish, with a few thyme leaves or snipped fresh chives if you like. (Only ever pick wild mushrooms with an experienced mushroom gatherer.)

Potato, Sage and Onion Soup

Serves   **4**
Prep   **15 mins**
Cook   **1 hour**

 Vegetarian

GF   Gluten-free

Sage and onion is a classic combination that works well in this thrifty, comforting potato soup inspired by a recipe created by the National Trust chefs.

1 tbsp vegetable oil

30g (1oz) butter

500g (1lb 2oz) onions, finely sliced

2 garlic cloves, chopped

2 tsp finely chopped fresh sage leaves

400g (14oz) floury potatoes, cut into small chunks

800ml (28fl oz) vegetable stock, plus extra if needed

2 tsp fresh thyme leaves, or 1 tsp dried thyme

150ml (5fl oz) milk, plus extra if needed

Salt and pepper

Sea salt flakes, to garnish

Crispy Onions (see Tip, page 160), to serve (optional)

Crispy fried sage

2 tbsp vegetable oil

1 tbsp butter (optional)

40 smallish fresh sage leaves

Heat the oil and butter in a large, heavy-based saucepan over a medium heat, add the onions and a pinch of salt, and cook for 8–10 minutes until softened. Turn the heat to low and cook for a further 20–30 minutes until really soft and golden, stirring occasionally.

Add the garlic and sage and cook for 1–2 minutes until aromatic. Stir in the potatoes, then add the stock and thyme, and bring to the boil. Reduce the heat, cover and simmer for 20 minutes or until the potatoes are tender.

Meanwhile, to make crispy fried sage, heat the oil and butter, if using, in a small pan over a medium-high heat. When it's hot, but not smoking, add the sage leaves and let them sizzle for a few seconds, then stir and fry for a few more seconds. Immediately remove with a slotted spoon and drain on kitchen paper.

Add the milk to the soup, then blitz the soup with a stick blender until smooth. Season to taste with salt and plenty of black pepper. Reheat gently, adding more stock or milk to adjust the consistency to your liking. Serve topped with crispy sage leaves and crispy onions, if you like, sprinkling the garnish with sea salt flakes.

Tip

To make this vegan, use an extra tablespoon of vegetable oil instead of butter and swap the dairy milk for oat or soya milk.

Curried Parsnip and Apple Soup

Serves	**4**
Prep	**20 mins**
Cook	**50 mins**

 Vegetarian

Food writer Jane Grigson invented curried parsnip soup around 50 years ago. It has become a modern classic, reinterpreted countless times. Mild curry powder best complements the sweetness of the parsnips, and this version includes tart apple for a touch of sharpness. There's no cream, yet the soup has a creamy taste from cooking the parsnips in butter. There's often no need to peel parsnips, but if you prefer to peel them you can use the peel to make parsnip crisps to serve with the soup.

500g (1lb 2oz) parsnips

3 tbsp butter

1 onion, roughly chopped

1 plump garlic clove, chopped

1 tsp mild curry powder

1 Granny Smith or small Bramley apple, peeled, cored and chopped

800ml (28fl oz) vegetable stock, plus extra if needed

½ tsp vegetable oil (for parsnip peel crisps)

A little milk, if needed

2–4 tbsp Greek-style yogurt, to taste, to serve (optional)

Pinch of cayenne pepper (optional)

Salt and pepper

If making parsnip peel crisps, preheat the oven to 150°C/130°C fan/gas 2. Scrub the parsnips and peel them, reserving the peel (you do not need to peel them if not making the crisps). Pat the peel dry with a clean tea towel and leave to dry out slightly while you prepare the vegetables.

Chop the parsnips into chunks. Melt the butter in a large saucepan, add the onion, garlic and parsnips, cover the pan and cook over a low heat for 10–15 minutes until the vegetables are golden and softened.

Add the curry powder and cook, stirring, for 2 minutes. Add the apple and some salt and pepper, and then add the stock and bring to the boil. Reduce the heat, partly cover the pan and simmer for 20–30 minutes until the parsnips are tender.

Meanwhile, if you have peeled the parsnips, place the peel in a bowl, add the oil and some salt and pepper, then mix with your fingers until all the peel is coated with oil. Spread the peel in a single layer on a baking sheet and bake for 15–20 minutes until browned – but don't let them burn. Transfer to a wire rack and leave to cool and crisp up.

Blitz the soup with a stick blender until it is very smooth. Taste and adjust the seasoning, and add a little water, milk or stock to adjust the consistency to your liking.

Reheat gently and serve. If you like, add a spoonful of yogurt and a tiny sprinkling of cayenne pepper. Serve the parsnip peel crisps on the side.

Tips

- Instead of homemade parsnip peel crisps, add crunch with garlicky Croutons (page 156) or lightly crushed poppadoms.
- Non-vegetarians might like to add a sprinkling of crisp frazzled bacon or Prosciutto Crisps (page 164).
- Alternatively, top with some diced apple tossed in lemon juice.
- Vegans could use oil instead of butter for the initial cooking of the veg and serve with plant-based yogurt.

Rosemary-Roasted Root Vegetable Soup

Serves **4**
Prep **20 mins**
Cook **1 hour**

 Vegan
GF Gluten-free

You can make this comforting soup with any odds and ends of root vegetables (see Tip). It's inspired by a soup created by the National Trust chefs to make the most of autumn vegetables from their kitchen gardens. This really benefits from a savoury crunchy topping, such as toasted seeds or shop-bought root vegetable crisps.

1 onion, cut into wedges

1 leek, cut into 6cm (2½in) pieces

1 celery stick, cut into 6cm (2½in) pieces

200g (7oz) swede, chopped into 3cm (1¼in) pieces

1 parsnip, chopped into 4cm (1½in) pieces

2 carrots, cut into 3cm (1¼in) chunks

2 garlic cloves, peeled

5 rosemary stalks

2 tbsp olive oil

800ml (28fl oz) vegetable stock, plus extra if needed

Juice of ½ lemon

Salt and pepper

To serve

2 tbsp oat cream

2 tbsp Toasted Seeds (page 158) or Garlic Breadcrumbs (page 157)

2 tbsp chopped fresh parsley

Preheat the oven to 200°C/180°C fan/gas 6. Put all the prepped vegetables, garlic and 3 of the rosemary stalks into a large roasting tin. Add the oil, some salt and pepper, and mix well. Roast for 30–45 minutes until the vegetables are just tender and beginning to brown at the edges.

Meanwhile, strip the leaves from the remaining rosemary stalks and chop finely.

Remove the roasted rosemary stalks from the roasting tin, then tip the contents of the tin into a large saucepan. Add 1 teaspoon of the chopped rosemary, or a little more to taste, pour in the stock and season with salt and pepper. Bring to the boil, then reduce the heat, cover and simmer for 5–10 minutes until the vegetables are soft.

Blitz the soup with a stick blender until smooth. Taste and adjust the seasoning, adding a squeeze of lemon juice to taste. Add a little extra stock or just-boiled water to adjust the consistency to your liking.

Reheat gently and serve with a swirl of oat cream, some toasted seeds and a sprinkling of parsley.

Tips

- To make this soup go further, add a tin of cannellini beans, black-eyed beans or chickpeas, rinsed and drained.
- You can substitute other root vegetables, such as celeriac, sweet potato, Jerusalem artichoke, pumpkin or butternut squash: you need a total of 800g (1¾lb) of vegetables. Beware of beetroot: it will take over the soup. Cut firmer veg into smaller pieces so that they roast evenly.

Jerusalem Artichoke Soup

Serves	**4**
Prep	**25 mins**
Cook	**35 mins**

V Vegetarian

GF Gluten-free

The season for Jerusalem artichokes is quite short – from about November to February – and this silky soup showcases their subtle, nutty flavour.

600g (1lb 5oz) Jerusalem artichokes

Juice of 1 lemon

30g (1oz) butter

1 onion, chopped

2 garlic cloves, chopped

1 potato, diced

800ml (28fl oz) vegetable stock

4 tbsp double cream, plus extra to serve

Salt and pepper

Freshly snipped chives or chopped fresh parsley, to garnish

To prepare the artichokes, put them in a bowl of salted water and give them a thorough scrub, then rinse in clean water. They shouldn't need peeling, although you may want to trim off a few discoloured bits. Have ready a bowl of water with the juice of about half the lemon. Slice the artichokes and drop them into the lemony water.

Melt the butter in a saucepan over a medium-low heat, add the onion and a good pinch of salt, and cook for 8–10 minutes until softened but not browned.

Add the garlic, potato and the drained artichokes, and stir well. Add the stock and bring to the boil. Reduce the heat, then cover and simmer for 10–20 minutes until the vegetables are tender.

Add a squeeze of lemon juice and leave to cool slightly. Blitz the soup with a stick blender until smooth, then rub it through a fine sieve. Be sure to scrape the bottom of the sieve to glean all the artichoke purée. Add the cream, taste and adjust the seasoning.

Reheat gently until hot and serve drizzled with extra cream and sprinkled with chives or parsley.

Tips

- Don't underestimate the time it will take to prepare the artichokes: they can be fiddly to scrub and trim, but you can do that an hour or two in advance. Once sliced, however, the artichokes discolour rapidly, and need to be kept in water with lemon juice for as short a time as possible.
- The artichokes' cooking time may vary depending on their age and size, and how thickly you slice them.

Broccoli, Stilton and Walnut Soup

Serves   **4**
Prep   **10 mins**
Cook   **20 mins**

Vegetarian

Gluten-free

This quick and easy soup is packed with nutrients from the broccoli, and it works out far cheaper per serving than ready-made versions. It's a great way to use leftover blue cheese and walnuts from a festive cheeseboard.

1 tbsp vegetable oil

1 onion or 1 bunch of spring onions, finely sliced

30g (1oz) walnuts

2 garlic cloves, chopped

700g (1lb 9oz) broccoli, finely chopped

800ml (28fl oz) vegetable stock

100ml (3½fl oz) single or double cream

150g (5½oz) Stilton or other blue cheese, crumbled, plus extra to serve

Salt and pepper

Heat the oil in a saucepan over a medium heat, add the onion and a pinch of salt, and cook for 8–10 minutes until softened.

Meanwhile, heat a small frying pan over a medium-high heat, add the walnuts and dry-fry, stirring often, for 2–3 minutes, until they begin to smell toasty. Tip onto a plate and leave to cool. Chop roughly.

Add the garlic and broccoli to the saucepan and stir well, then turn up the heat to high and pour in the stock, add a little salt and pepper, and bring to the boil. Reduce the heat, then cover and simmer for 5 minutes or until the broccoli is just tender.

Add most of the cream (reserving a little to garnish) and the Stilton, then blitz the soup using a stick blender until smooth. Taste and adjust the seasoning.

Reheat gently and serve topped with a swirl of cream, some crumbled Stilton and the chopped toasted walnuts.

Tips

- Chop the broccoli finely (or blitz it in a food processor), so that it cooks quickly and keeps its green colour. To use the broccoli stalk, peel off the tough outer layer before chopping.
- If you can't eat nuts, replace the walnuts with Croutons (page 156).
- You can toast and chop the walnuts up to 2 days in advance: keep them in an airtight container in a cool, dark place.

Pulses, Pasta and Grains

Puls was a staple food in ancient Rome. Its main ingredient was farro, a type of wheat, sometimes with the addition of broad beans, making this a completely nutritious one-pot meal. Extra flavour came from vegetables, herbs, cheese, meat or one of the Romans' pungent sauces. The word 'pulses', that we use today for dried legumes, comes from this staple.

Until relatively recent times, dried peas, beans, chickpeas and lentils took the place of meat in the bowls of the poor. Along with grains such as barley and oats, pulses could be stored for long periods, to be added to the pot when needed. As complex carbohydrates they provide energy and fibre to fill the belly; they are also high in protein, calcium and other nutrients. Unlike animal products such as fish, meat and cheese, pulses are not considered 'complete proteins', but in combination with a grain – such as pasta, noodles, rice or bread – they provide all that the body needs.

In East Asia, the staple pulse was the versatile soya bean. As well as being used in its natural state, for thousands of years it has also been processed to make tofu, soy sauce and miso (fermented soya bean paste). Unlike other pulses, soya beans are considered a complete protein.

White, red, black and runner beans were among the foods introduced to Europe from the Americas in the 16th century, along with tomatoes, peppers, maize, potatoes and chocolate. People welcomed the new beans and soon developed varieties such as borlotti and cannellini.

Although dried beans need soaking, in theory it is unnecessary for dried lentils and split peas (but check the packet); however, I like to let them sit in their rinsing water for about 30 minutes before giving them a final rinse – it seems to help them cook more quickly and evenly. Dried lentils are fairly quick to cook; dried green and yellow split peas take a little longer. In some recipes I use tinned beans and chickpeas for convenience. They are not expensive, although if you use a lot of these pulses you may find it more economical to use the dried versions. You need to soak them overnight and then simmer them for at least an hour or two, but they can be cooked in bulk and kept in the fridge for up to three days or frozen for up to three months in some of their cooking liquid. A pressure cooker, instant pot or slow cooker makes it energy efficient to cook beans and chickpeas. Adding a bay leaf to the water when you cook them results in a flavoursome stock, so don't pour it away: you can tailor it to any soup by adding some peelings from the veg you're using.

This chapter focuses on substantial vegetarian and vegan soups. In a few of the recipes, meat is used sparingly, just lending its flavour to the pot, as it would traditionally have been, but you can easily make these soups without meat.

Broad Bean Minestrone

Serves **4**
Prep **15 mins**
Cook **40 mins**

 Vegan

This pretty soup, developed by the National Trust chefs, showcases the vegetables that appear in late spring and early summer. You need only a small amount of each vegetable, so it's perfect if your allotment hasn't produced the abundant harvest you were hoping for. For the best flavour, you will need a good, preferably homemade, vegetable stock. You can swap in other vegetables: asparagus (cut into 2cm (¾in) pieces), peas, runner beans (strings removed and cut into 2cm (¾in) slices), fennel (sliced thinly), diced courgette or new potatoes.

1 tbsp olive oil

1 onion, chopped

2 carrots, diced

2 celery sticks, diced

2 garlic cloves, finely chopped

1.2 litres (2 pints) vegetable stock

1 bay leaf

70g (2½oz) spaghetti, broken into short lengths

140g (5oz) green beans, cut into 3cm (1¼in) lengths

140g (5oz) broad beans, podded (fresh or frozen)

55g (2oz) green cabbage, chopped

4 tsp vegan Pesto (page 154), plus extra to serve

Extra virgin olive oil and/or fresh basil leaves to garnish (optional)

Salt and pepper

Heat the oil in a saucepan over a medium heat, add the onion, carrots, celery and a pinch of salt, and cook for 10 minutes or until softened.

Add the garlic and cook for 1 minute. Add the stock, bay leaf and a little salt and pepper, and bring to the boil. Reduce the heat, cover and simmer for 15 minutes or until the vegetables are soft.

Add the broken spaghetti, bring back to the boil and cook for 5 minutes or until the pasta is just tender.

Add the green beans, broad beans and cabbage, then stir the pesto through the soup and cook for 3 minutes.

Remove the bay leaf, taste and adjust the seasoning and serve hot. Garnish with a drizzle of extra virgin olive oil and a few basil leaves, if you like, and add extra pesto to taste.

Tips

- If using fresh broad beans in their pods, you'll need to start with about 300g (10½oz). You can add the pods to the stock before you start the recipe and simmer for 10 minutes while the onions are softening, then strain and use in this soup – or save the pods to add to your next batch of vegetable stock.

- If using fresh broad beans, you can remove the outer casing around each bean for a brighter green colour in the soup.

- This soup is best served soon after making so that the green vegetables stay bright green. Add the vegetables according to the time they take to cook: for example, if you include diced new potatoes, add them when you add the stock; if you include asparagus, it will need only 2 minutes cooking time.

- If you're not vegan or vegetarian, you could begin by frying 50g (1¾oz) diced bacon or pancetta for a few minutes before the onion.

Soupe au Pistou

Serves	**4–6**
Prep	**20 mins, plus overnight soaking**
Cook	**1¾–2¼ hours**

V Vegetarian

Fragrant with garlic and basil, this Provençal soup sings of summer. In France it is often made with semi-dried white haricot beans harvested in late summer, although it can be made throughout the year whenever fresh basil is available, and using dried white haricot beans and seasonal vegetables, such as chopped leeks or celery, sliced fennel, diced celeriac, small turnips, carrots or pumpkin.

150g (5½oz) dried haricot beans, soaked overnight

1 bay leaf

3 garlic cloves, peeled: 1 whole, 2 finely chopped

2 ripe tomatoes, skinned, deseeded (see method) and chopped

1 large onion, chopped

140g (5oz) new potatoes, scrubbed and diced

2 courgettes, cut into thick slices then quartered

60g (2¼oz) small macaroni, small shell pasta or other soup pasta

140g (5oz) green beans or runner beans (stringed), cut into 2cm (¾in) pieces

100g (3½oz) fresh or frozen peas

Salt and pepper

Finely grated Gruyère, Parmesan or vegetarian alternative to serve

Pistou

2 garlic cloves, peeled

¼ tsp coarse sea salt

Bunch of basil leaves, about 30g (1oz)

4 tbsp olive oil

1 ripe tomato, skinned, deseeded and chopped

30g (1oz) Gruyère, Parmesan or vegetarian alternative, finely grated

Drain and rinse the beans, then put them in a large saucepan with the bay leaf and the whole garlic clove, and add about 1.2 litres (2 pints) cold water to cover them. Bring to a rapid boil for 10 minutes, then reduce the heat to a very gentle simmer and cook for 1–1½ hours, shaking the pan occasionally, until the beans are tender. You may need to top up with boiling water from time to time. To test, squash a cooled bean between your finger and thumb: there should be no hint of chalkiness.

If you like, you can use the bean cooking liquid to peel the tomatoes (including the one for the pistou): lower them into the simmering liquid for 30–60 seconds, then lift them out using a slotted spoon and place in a bowl of cold water. Within 1 minute or so they will be cool enough to handle and the skins will peel off easily. Cut them in half and squeeze out the seeds, then roughly chop them.

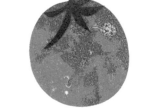

While the beans are cooking, make the pistou: in a pestle and mortar, pound the garlic with the salt and basil until fairly smooth. Gradually drizzle in half the olive oil, then pound in the tomato and cheese, then the remaining olive oil. Alternatively, put all the ingredients into a blender and pulse to make a paste. Transfer to a small serving bowl. If you want to keep the pistou overnight, pour a thin layer of olive oil over the surface and store in the fridge.

Remove and discard the bay leaf and garlic clove from the beans. Add the onion and chopped garlic to the beans, along with 1 teaspoon of salt, and simmer for 10 minutes. Add the potatoes, tomatoes and courgettes, and simmer for a further 10 minutes.

Add the pasta, green beans and peas, then bring back to the boil and cook for 10 minutes until the pasta is tender.

Taste and adjust the seasoning, adding plenty of black pepper. Ladle the hot soup into bowls. Add a spoonful of pistou to each bowl and serve the rest separately, along with some extra cheese to sprinkle over the soup.

Tip

Parmesan and Gruyère are traditional, but some Provençal recipes use a hard Dutch cheese such as mature Edam (not the rubbery, plastic-wrapped stuff) – so why not try mature Cheddar in this soup?

Black Bean Soup with Charred Tomato Salsa

Serves **4**
Prep **20 mins**
Cook **30 mins**

V Vegetarian
GF Gluten-free

This Latin American soup is very popular in the United States. You can get creative with the garnishes and accompaniments: try diced avocado, sweetcorn, chopped spring onion or red onion.

1 tbsp vegetable oil

1 large onion, diced

1 large carrot, diced

1 celery stick, diced

1 green pepper, deseeded and diced

2 garlic cloves, chopped

1½ tsp ground cumin

½–1 tsp chilli powder, to taste

1 tsp dried oregano

2 x 400g (14oz) tins black beans, drained

600ml (1 pint) vegetable stock

Juice of ½ lime

Salt and pepper

To serve

4 tbsp soured cream

2 tbsp roughly chopped fresh coriander

1 lime, cut into wedges

Tortilla chips

Charred tomato salsa

4 plum tomatoes

1 jalapeño chilli

1 garlic clove

3 spring onions, finely chopped

2 tbsp roughly chopped fresh coriander

Juice of ½ lime

Pinch of sea salt flakes

Pinch of sugar, or to taste

First, make the tomato salsa: heat a heavy frying pan over a high heat. Add the tomatoes, chilli and garlic, and cook, turning from time to time, until charred and soft. Leave in the pan to cool for 10 minutes. Slit the chilli and remove the seeds and stem; slip the garlic out of its skin. Chop the tomatoes, chilli and garlic together, or blitz briefly, then tip into a bowl and stir in the spring onions and coriander. Add lime juice, sea salt and a pinch of sugar to taste.

To make the soup, heat the oil in a large saucepan, add the onion, carrot, celery, green pepper and a pinch of salt, and cook for 8–10 minutes until softened.

Add the garlic, cumin, chilli powder, oregano and beans, stir for 2–3 minutes, then add the stock. Bring to the boil, then reduce the heat, cover and simmer for 15 minutes or until the vegetables are soft.

Remove 6 tablespoons of the vegetable mixture and set aside. Blitz the soup until smooth, then return the unblended vegetables to the pan. Taste and adjust the seasoning, adding lime juice to lift the flavour. Serve with a spoonful of soured cream, with coriander scattered over; serve lime wedges, tortilla chips and the tomato salsa in small bowls for people to help themselves.

Tips

• Veganise this soup by replacing the soured cream with a plant-based cream or yogurt alternative.

• You can make the soup and salsa in advance, but don't add the lime juice until just before serving.

66

Miso Ramen

Serves **4**
Prep **20 mins**
Cook **25 mins**

 Vegetarian

It began as a noodle soup for workers in Japan, but ramen is now a global foodie phenomenon. It can be a complex dish with a broth made from pork bones simmered for many hours, added to a *tare*, or seasoning base, with toppings in infinite variety, but it should always be full of savoury umami flavour – and slurped while it's steaming hot. Try this simple vegetarian version – you'll find it much easier if you weigh and prep all the ingredients before you start cooking.

- 20g (¾oz) dried shiitake mushrooms
- 1.2 litres (2 pints) vegetable stock or water
- 3cm (1¼in) piece of fresh ginger, peeled and grated
- 3–4 garlic cloves, to taste, grated
- 3 tbsp soy sauce
- 2 tbsp mirin (Japanese rice wine)
- 6 spring onions, sliced, keeping white and green parts separate
- 250g (9oz) dried ramen or udon noodles
- 2 eggs, at room temperature
- 1 tbsp sesame oil
- 150g (5½oz) fresh shiitake mushrooms, cut into thick slices if large
- 2 small pak choi, quartered lengthways
- 3 tbsp miso
- 1 tbsp sesame seeds, toasted
- 1 fresh red chilli, deseeded and finely sliced, or hot chilli sauce, to taste
- Salt and ground white pepper

Put the dried mushrooms in a large saucepan and pour in the stock. Add the ginger, half the garlic, half the soy sauce and mirin, and the green part of the spring onions. Bring to the boil, then reduce the heat, cover and simmer for 20 minutes or until the mushrooms are tender.

If using whole dried shiitake, lift them out of the broth, cut off and discard the hard stems, slice the mushrooms and put them back in the broth. Taste the broth and add more soy sauce and mirin if you like, along with a pinch of salt and white pepper. The broth must be well flavoured because the noodles will take up the flavour, although the miso (added later) will add extra flavour.

While the stock is simmering, cook the noodles in boiling water according to the packet instructions. Drain in a colander and rinse under cold water until cold. Leave in the colander.

Meanwhile, boil the kettle. Pour the boiling water into the pan in which you cooked the noodles, lower in the eggs and cook for 6½ minutes. Drain and lift them into a bowl of cold water until cool enough to handle. Peel the eggs and slice in half.

—continued overleaf

Rinse the pan, then put over a medium-high heat and add the sesame oil, the remaining garlic and the white parts of the spring onions, and stir-fry for 30 seconds. Add the fresh mushrooms and stir-fry for 2–3 minutes until cooked and fragrant. Season to taste with a pinch of salt.

Add the pak choi to the simmering broth and cook for 2–3 minutes until the pak choi is just tender.

In a small bowl, mix the miso with a little of the hot broth until smooth, then stir it back into the hot broth.

Divide the noodles between four warmed deep bowls. Ladle the hot broth over the noodles. Top with the stir-fried mushrooms, halved eggs, a sprinkling of sesame seeds and sliced chilli or hot chilli sauce, to taste.

Tips

- When cooking with miso, it's important not to let it boil: stir it into the hot broth near to the end of the cooking time.
- For this simple veggie ramen, you can use any style of miso, or a combination of two styles for additional layers of flavour: white miso is the mildest; red miso is saltier and more pungent; brown miso is deeper in flavour.
- Instead of the pak choi, try thinly sliced broccoli florets. You could also add sliced bamboo shoots, beansprouts, sweetcorn, edamame, or a sheet of dried nori seaweed.
- If you like, use a mix of black and white sesame seeds, or white sesame seeds and nigella seeds.

Laksa

Serves **4**
Prep **30 mins**
Cook **25 mins**

 Vegan
GF Gluten-free

Found throughout South-East Asia, with countless variations, laksa is a coconut curry soup with noodles. It's often made with chicken, pork or prawns, but this vegan version is brimful of noodles, beansprouts, crunchy peanuts and crispy fried tofu.

400g (14oz) cauliflower

600ml (1 pint) vegetable stock

½ tsp soft brown sugar, plus extra if needed

2 kaffir (makrut) lime leaves, torn in half (optional)

400ml (14fl oz) full-fat coconut milk

170g (6oz) beansprouts, rinsed in cold water and drained

170g (6oz) green beans, cut into 3cm (1¼in) lengths

170g (6oz) rice noodles

Juice of 1 lime

Salt

Laksa paste

4 tsp vegetable oil

70g (2½oz) shallots, roughly chopped

2 lemongrass stalks, outer layer removed, finely chopped

5cm (2in) piece of fresh ginger, about 15g (½oz), peeled and grated

3 garlic cloves, grated

1–2 fresh red chillies, to taste, deseeded and chopped

1 tsp ground coriander

1 tsp ground turmeric

1 tsp ground cumin

Crispy tofu

200g (7oz) firm tofu, drained

2 tbsp cornflour

2 tbsp vegetable oil

Toppings

6 spring onions, thinly sliced

Handful of fresh coriander leaves

4 tbsp roasted peanuts, roughly chopped

Crispy Shallots (page 160)

4 lime wedges

Tips

- Instead of the cauliflower, try butternut squash, pumpkin or sweet potato cut into 2cm (¾in) cubes.
- Instead of green beans you could use mangetout: blanch them for 1 minute.
- If gluten is not a problem for you, you could use egg noodles instead of rice noodles.
- If you're not vegetarian or vegan, you could add some Thai fish sauce when seasoning the coconut soup.

First, make the laksa paste: put half the oil and all the remaining ingredients into a food processor with a pinch of salt, and blend to a paste. Heat the remaining oil in a large saucepan over a medium heat and fry the spice paste for 3–4 minutes until fragrant, stirring frequently so that it cooks but doesn't burn.

To make the crispy tofu, pat the tofu as dry as you can with a clean tea towel, then put on a plate and cover with another plate with a weight on top (such as a tin of beans). Leave to dry out while you start to make the soup.

Cut the cauliflower into small florets and cut the stem into thin slices. Add the stock to the laksa paste along with the cauliflower, sugar and lime leaves, if using, and bring to the boil. Reduce the heat, add the coconut milk, and simmer gently, uncovered, for 15 minutes or until just tender.

Meanwhile, cut the tofu into 2cm (¾in) cubes and toss with the cornflour and a good pinch of salt to coat evenly. Heat the oil in a non-stick frying pan over a medium-high heat and fry the tofu, turning gently until golden all over. Drain on kitchen paper.

Blanch the beansprouts in a saucepan of boiling water for 15 seconds; remove with a slotted spoon, refresh in cold water and drain. Bring the water back to the boil and blanch the green beans for 3 minutes or until just tender; remove with a slotted spoon, refresh in cold water and drain.

Cook the noodles according to the packet instructions. Drain well and divide among four deep bowls.

Add most of the lime juice to the coconut soup, then taste and add more lime juice, salt or sugar to get a good, strong balance of flavours.

To serve, add the green beans and beansprouts to the bowls. Ladle the hot coconut soup over the vegetables. Top with the spring onions, fresh coriander, peanuts, crispy tofu and crispy shallots, and serve immediately with lime wedges to squeeze over.

Spelt and Borlotti Bean Soup

Serves   **4–6**
Prep   **20 mins, plus overnight soaking if using dried beans**
Cook   **1½–2 hours**

 Vegan
GF   Gluten-free

Both spelt and borlotti beans are increasingly being grown in Britain. If you see borlotti beans at a farmers' market in late summer or early autumn, you'll find it hard to resist the marbled pink-and-cream pods. They contain pale beans splashed with magenta, and they keep their colour when dried but turn brown when cooked.

Farro is the name used in Italy for any of three ancient species of wheat: emmer, einkorn and spelt. Based on a rustic Italian soup, *minestra di farro e fagioli*, this one-pot dish is very nutritious, especially if you add rocket and cheese on top.

1kg (2lb 3oz) fresh (semi-dried) borlotti beans in their pods, or 200g (7oz) dried borlotti beans, soaked overnight

2 bay leaves

2 tbsp olive oil

1 onion, finely chopped

1 carrot, finely chopped

1 celery stick, finely chopped

4 garlic cloves, finely chopped

1½ tsp finely chopped fresh rosemary

10 fresh sage leaves, finely chopped

¼ tsp dried chilli flakes (optional)

1 tbsp tomato purée

1 litre (1¾ pints) vegetable stock – use the cooking liquid from the beans, adding vegetable stock to make up to 1 litre (1¾ pints)

150g (5½oz) pearled spelt, rinsed

Salt and pepper

Extra virgin olive oil, to serve

If using dried soaked borlotti beans, drain and rinse them, then put them in a saucepan with the bay leaves and add cold water to cover them by 3cm (1¼in). Bring to a rapid boil for 10 minutes, then reduce the heat to a very gentle simmer and cook for 1–2 hours until the beans are soft but not overcooked and mushy, shaking the pan occasionally. You may need to top up with boiling water. To test, squash a cooled bean between your finger and thumb: there should be no hint of chalkiness. When they're done, drain the beans, reserving the cooking liquid, and discard the bay leaves.

If using fresh (semi-dried) borlotti beans, pop them out of their pods and put them in a saucepan of boiling water with the bay leaves. Bring to the boil and boil for 10 minutes, then reduce the heat and simmer for 30–40 minutes until tender. Drain, reserving the cooking liquid, and discard the bay leaves.

Heat the oil in a large saucepan, add the onion, carrot, celery, garlic, rosemary, sage and chilli, if using, and cook for 5 minutes. Add the tomato purée and cook for a further 2 minutes.

Add the reserved cooking liquid/stock and bring to the boil, then add the spelt and beans. Reduce the heat and cook at a steady simmer for 25–40 minutes, until the spelt grains are tender.

Remove about two-thirds of the soup and set aside. Blitz the remaining third with a stick blender until smooth. Return the unblended soup to the pan and season with plenty of salt and freshly ground black pepper. Reheat gently. To serve, top with a drizzle of extra virgin olive oil.

Tips

- If you're really short of time you could use 2 x 400g (14oz) tins borlotti beans, drained and rinsed. Add them when the spelt is tender, then simmer for a further 10 minutes.
- If you like, top with a handful of rocket and some shaved pecorino cheese (or vegan alternative) before drizzling with olive oil.
- Add extra flavour by stirring in 85g (3oz) roughly chopped sun-dried or semi-dried tomatoes.
- The original rustic soup would, whenever possible, have included a prosciutto bone or a small piece of ham or ham fat. If you eat meat, you could add 100g (3½oz) finely chopped unsmoked pancetta when cooking the onion mixture.
- If you can't find pearled spelt, use pearl barley; it might take up to 1 hour to become really tender.
- This soup will need plenty of seasoning, but don't add salt until the soup is nearly done, as it may cause the beans to toughen.

Roasted Carrot, Harissa and Chickpea Soup with Tahini Yogurt

Serves **4**
Prep **35 mins**
Cook **35 mins**

 Vegan

 Gluten-free

Sweet carrots, fiery harissa and a cooling, lemony tahini dressing make a bowlful of goodness for lunch or supper. Great on its own, or it can be topped with crispy chickpeas, fresh mint or coriander and a sprinkling of sesame seeds, and served with warm, soft flatbreads.

500g (1lb 2oz) carrots, cut into small chunks

4–6 tbsp harissa, to taste

4 tsp vegetable oil

1 tbsp maple syrup

2 garlic cloves, finely chopped

1 onion, finely chopped

800ml (28fl oz) vegetable stock

400g (14oz) tin chickpeas

Crispy Chickpeas (page 161)

Sesame seeds, to serve (optional)

Small fresh mint or coriander leaves, to serve (optional)

Salt and pepper

Tahini yogurt

3 tbsp plant-based yogurt

1½ tbsp tahini

Grated zest and juice of ½ lemon

Preheat the oven to 200°C/180°C fan/gas 6. Put the carrots in a bowl, add 3 tablespoons of the harissa, half the oil, the maple syrup and garlic, and mix well. Tip the carrots into the roasting tin and roast for 20 minutes or until just tender, stirring halfway through.

Meanwhile, to make the tahini yogurt, put the ingredients in a bowl and mix until smooth. Season with salt and pepper to taste and add a little water to achieve the consistency of thick pouring cream.

Heat the remaining oil in a large saucepan, add the onion and a pinch of salt, and cook for 5 minutes or until softened. Tip the roasted carrots into the saucepan. Pour a little of the stock into the roasting tin and stir to dislodge the roasting juices, then add to the saucepan, along with the remaining stock and the tin of chickpeas, including their liquid. Bring to the boil, then reduce the heat, cover and simmer for 5–10 minutes until the chickpeas are hot.

Remove about two-thirds of the soup. Blitz with a stick blender until smooth, then return to the pan. Taste and adjust the seasoning, adding more harissa to suit your taste.

To serve, drizzle with the tahini yogurt and scatter with some of the crispy chickpeas, adding sesame seeds and a few mint leaves if you like.

Tips

- If you are not vegan you could use dairy yogurt, and honey instead of maple syrup.
- Any leftover crispy chickpeas make a great snack; store in an airtight container for up to 5 days.

Lentil, Spinach and Noodle Soup

Serves	**4–6**
Prep	**20 mins**
Cook	**50 mins–1 hour 5 mins**

 Vegetarian

The inspiration for this dish is a herb-packed Persian soup-stew that often includes chickpeas or beans as well as lentils and noodles. Feel free to add them to this hearty meal in a bowl. Note: if making this for six, use the larger amounts of spinach, lentils, stock and noodles.

250–300g (9–10½oz) fresh spinach leaves

50g (1¾oz) spring onions

20g (¾oz) fresh parsley

20g (¾oz) fresh coriander

10g (⅓oz) fresh mint leaves

170–200g (6–7oz) green or brown lentils

1 tbsp olive oil

2 onions, finely chopped

3 garlic cloves, finely chopped

1 tsp ground turmeric

¼ tsp freshly ground black pepper

1.2–1.5 litres (2–2½ pints) vegetable stock, plus extra if needed

100–150g (3½–5½oz) long noodles, such as spaghetti, roughly broken

Salt

To serve

150g (5½oz) soured cream or crème fraîche

Crispy Shallots (page 160)

Weigh out your spinach, spring onions and herbs, rinse and leave them to drain. Weigh out and rinse your lentils, then leave them to soak while you cook the onions.

Heat the oil in a large saucepan over a medium heat, add the onions, garlic and a pinch of salt, and cook for 8–10 minutes until softened.

Add the turmeric and pepper and cook for 1 minute. Drain the lentils, add them to the saucepan and stir briefly. Add the stock and bring to the boil, then reduce the heat slightly, cover and simmer for 30–40 minutes until the lentils are tender.

Add the noodles and cook for 10–15 minutes until just tender.

Meanwhile, chop the spinach, spring onions and herbs. Add them to the soup, stirring until they wilt. Taste and adjust the seasoning, and add a little more stock or just-boiled water to adjust the consistency to your liking.

Serve topped with a generous spoonful of soured cream and some crispy shallots.

Tips

- Use a food processor to chop the spinach, spring onions and herbs together.
- If you have some leftover cooked or tinned chickpeas, black-eyed peas, pinto beans or red kidney beans, you could add them when you add the noodles.
- Instead of crispy shallots you could make a caramelised onion topping: heat 30g (1oz) butter in a small saucepan until it foams, add two thinly sliced onions and cook over a low heat for 20–30 minutes, stirring from time to time, until dark brown and caramelised.

Red Lentil, Chickpea and Fresh Coriander Soup

Serves **4**
Prep **10 mins**
Cook **40 mins**

 Vegan
GF Gluten-free

Deeply savoury and satisfying, this soup ticks all the boxes: it's simple, inexpensive and nutritious. It was created by the National Trust chefs.

20g (¾oz) fresh coriander, stalks and leaves separated

1 tbsp vegetable oil

1 onion, chopped

2 tbsp tikka masala paste (see Tip)

200g (7oz) red lentils, rinsed

1.2 litres (2 pints) vegetable stock

400g (14oz) tin chickpeas, drained

Salt and pepper

Reserve the coriander leaves and finely chop the stalks. Heat the oil in a saucepan over a medium heat, add the onion, coriander stalks and a pinch of salt, and cook for 5 minutes.

Add the tikka masala paste and cook, stirring, for 2–3 minutes until fragrant. Add the lentils and the stock. Bring to the boil, then partly cover the pan, reduce the heat and simmer for 30 minutes or until the lentils are soft, stirring from time to time.

Roughly chop the reserved coriander leaves.

Blitz the soup with a stick blender until smooth. Add most of the coriander leaves and the chickpeas, then taste and adjust the seasoning. Bring back to the boil. Serve in bowls and scatter the remaining coriander leaves on top.

Tips

- Not all tikka masala paste is vegan, so check the label when you shop.
- You could add a handful of Crispy Chickpeas (page 161) for a crunchy garnish.

Serves **4**
Prep **10 mins**
Cook **25 mins**

(V∅) Vegan
(GF) Gluten-free

Curried White Bean Soup with Wilted Spinach and Chilli Oil

Super-healthy and hearty, this soup is perfect for lunch or supper. If you're out to impress vegan friends, add a drizzle of vegan cream as well as the chilli oil, and finish with some shards of plain poppadom – added at the last minute so that they don't go soggy.

1 tbsp vegetable oil

1 large onion, finely chopped

2 garlic cloves, finely chopped

2cm (¾in) fresh ginger, peeled and grated

1 tsp ground cumin

½ tsp ground coriander

½ tsp ground turmeric

¼ tsp chilli powder or cayenne

¼ tsp ground fenugreek or cardamom

2 x 400g (14oz) tins cannellini or white haricot beans, drained

600ml (1 pint) vegetable stock

Good pinch of garam masala (optional)

Squeeze of lemon juice (optional)

100g (3½oz) young spinach leaves

Salt and pepper

Chilli oil

2 tbsp olive oil

Pinch of dried chilli flakes

¼ tsp paprika

Heat the oil in a large saucepan over a medium-low heat, add the onion and a pinch of salt, and cook for 10 minutes or until softened.

Meanwhile, make the chilli oil: put the oil in a small pan, add the chilli flakes and put over a medium-low heat for 3–4 minutes. Stir in the paprika and a tiny pinch of salt. Remove from the heat and set aside.

Add the garlic to the onion in the pan, with the ginger, spices, a good pinch of salt and plenty of black pepper. Stir and cook for 1 minute. Add the beans and cook, stirring occasionally, for 2–3 minutes. Add the stock, bring to the boil, then reduce the heat, cover and simmer for 10 minutes.

Remove half the contents of the pan. Blitz with a stick blender until smooth, then return it to the pan. Taste and adjust the seasoning, adding garam masala and/or lemon juice if needed.

Bring back to the boil, then add the spinach and stir until just wilted. Serve drizzled with the chilli oil.

Tips

- For a quick and easy variation, replace the spices with ready-mixed curry powder.
- You can make the bean soup in advance, but reheat and add the spinach just before serving.

Chickpeas and Spinach in Tomato and Saffron Broth

Serves **4**
Prep **15 mins**
Cook **30 mins**

 Vegetarian

GF Gluten-free

A fragrant saffron broth, made with good, ripe summer tomatoes, is the secret behind this simple rustic soup. Serve with bread and add a poached or fried egg if you fancy it.

2 tbsp olive oil

1 large onion, finely chopped

2 garlic cloves, finely chopped

Good pinch of saffron strands

400g (14oz) ripe tomatoes, skinned, deseeded (see Tip) and chopped

400g (14oz) tin chickpeas, drained and rinsed

600ml (1 pint) vegetable stock

400g (14oz) fresh spinach, tough stems removed, leaves shredded

Salt and pepper

4 poached or fried eggs, to serve (optional)

Heat the oil in a large saucepan over a medium heat, add the onion and a pinch of salt, and cook for 10 minutes or until softened.

Add the garlic and saffron and cook for 1 minute. Add the tomatoes and another pinch of salt and cook for 3 minutes, stirring.

Add the chickpeas and stock. Bring to the boil, then reduce the heat, cover and simmer for 10 minutes.

Stir in the spinach and cook until just wilted. Taste and adjust the seasoning. Serve in soup plates, adding a poached or fried egg if you like.

Tips

• To skin and deseed the tomatoes, cut a small cross at the base of each, then place in a bowl, pour over boiling water to cover and leave for 30 seconds. Drain and immediately put them in a bowl of ice-cold water. The skins should now peel off easily. Cut the tomatoes in half and squeeze out the seeds.

• No need to waste these tomato trimmings: add them to the vegetable stock and bring to the boil for a few minutes while the onion is softening, then strain the stock through a fine sieve and use as above.

Vegetarian

Ribollita

The name of this Tuscan soup means 'reboiled' and it is even better if made a day ahead and then reheated, with the kale added shortly before serving. Cavolo nero, or Tuscan black kale, is a hardy plant that can be harvested throughout the winter as a reliable food source. Ribollita is a delicious way to use up slightly stale bread.

2 tbsp olive oil

1 onion, finely chopped

2 carrots, diced

2 celery sticks, diced

3 garlic cloves, peeled: 1 halved, 2 finely chopped

½ tsp fennel seeds, crushed

¼ tsp dried chilli flakes

400g (14oz) tin chopped tomatoes

800ml (28fl oz) vegetable stock

1 bay leaf

Piece of rind from a hard cheese such as Parmesan, pecorino or a vegetarian alternative (optional)

2 x 400g (14oz) tins cannellini or borlotti beans, drained

200g (7oz) cavolo nero, shredded

4 thick slices day-old rustic-style bread

Salt and pepper

To serve

Extra virgin olive oil

Grated Parmesan, pecorino (or vegetarian alternative) or mature Cheddar

Heat the oil in a large saucepan over a medium heat, add the onion, carrots, celery and a pinch of salt, and cook for 10 minutes or until softened.

Add the chopped garlic, fennel seeds and chilli, and cook for 2 minutes. Add the tomatoes, stock, bay leaf, Parmesan rind (or vegetarian alternative), if using, and a little salt and pepper, and bring to the boil. Cover and simmer for 30 minutes.

Add the beans and return to the boil, then reduce the heat, cover and simmer for a further 15 minutes. If making a day ahead, cool the soup quickly at this stage and store in the fridge.

To serve, bring the soup back to the boil, add the cavolo nero and simmer for 10 minutes or until tender.

Meanwhile, lightly toast the bread and rub with the halved garlic. Put a slice of bread in each soup plate. Use a slotted spoon to lift the cheese rind out of the soup and remove the bay leaf. Taste the soup and adjust the seasoning, then ladle over the bread in the soup plates. Drizzle over some extra virgin olive oil and sprinkle a little grated cheese on top. Serve extra grated cheese separately in a small bowl.

Tips

- If you can't get cavolo nero, substitute any kale, green cabbage or chard.
- You can add odds and ends from the fridge, such as leftover cooked squash, potatoes or other vegetables, to heat through before serving.
- If you like, add a handful or two of pasta or rice to the soup along with the cavolo nero.
- If you're not vegetarian, you could begin by frying 85g (3oz) finely diced bacon or pancetta with the onions.

Lentil, Bacon and Leek Soup with Mint and Whipped Feta

Serves **4**
Prep **15 mins**
Cook **1 hour**

GF Gluten-free

A chunky, everyday lentil soup, made fresh and bright with the addition of green leeks, mint and tangy whipped feta.

1 tbsp vegetable oil

150g (5½oz) smoked bacon lardons or thick rashers, diced

1 large onion, finely chopped

2 carrots, diced

1 celery stick, diced (optional)

2 garlic cloves, sliced

2 thyme sprigs

200g (7oz) green or brown lentils, rinsed

1 litre (1¾ pints) ham, chicken or vegetable stock, plus extra if needed

300g (10½oz) leeks, sliced

1 lemon, halved

Salt and pepper

Whipped feta

100g (3½oz) feta cheese

5 tbsp Greek-style yogurt

To serve

Leaves from 5–6 mint sprigs, or more, to taste

Extra virgin olive oil

Heat the oil in a large saucepan over a medium heat, add the bacon and fry until lightly browned. Add the onion, carrots and celery, if using, and cook for 8–10 minutes until softened.

Add the garlic, thyme and lentils, and stir to mix with the vegetables. Add the stock and bring to the boil for 5 minutes, then reduce the heat, cover and simmer for 30 minutes or until the lentils are soft.

Meanwhile, to make the whipped feta, put the feta and yogurt in a food processor or blender and blitz until smooth.

Take the leaves off the mint sprigs. Pile the leaves on top of each other, roll them up tightly and cut into thin strips – don't do this too far in advance or the mint will discolour.

Blitz roughly half of the soup in the pan using a stick blender.

Tip

For a vegetarian version, leave out the bacon and add ½–1 teaspoon smoked paprika to the onion, carrots and celery.

Bring back to the boil. Add the leeks, season with salt and pepper, and simmer for 5 minutes or until the leeks are just tender. Taste and adjust the seasoning, adding a good squeeze of lemon juice, and add a little more stock or just-boiled water to adjust the consistency to your liking.

Serve topped with the whipped feta, a scattering of mint and a drizzle of extra virgin olive oil.

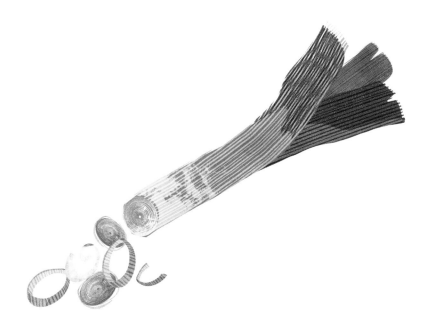

Split Pea and Ham Soup

Serves **4–6**
Prep **15 mins, plus soaking**
Cook **about 3 hours**

 Gluten-free

A popular soup in 19th-century London, split pea and ham soup was sometimes called London Particular, which was also the name for the notorious thick, yellowish 'pea souper' smog that regularly blanketed industrial London until the Clean Air Act of 1956. This version uses inexpensive ham hock to make a wonderfully warming soup.

1 gammon (uncooked ham) hock
300g (10½oz) yellow or green split peas
1 large onion, quartered
2 carrots, roughly chopped
1 celery stick, roughly chopped
10 peppercorns
2 bay leaves
4 thyme sprigs
4 parsley sprigs
Salt and pepper

Tips

- Soaking the split peas helps them to cook more quickly and evenly. Read the packet instructions, because some split peas need longer soaking.
- Use unsmoked or smoked ham hock. Soaking the hock helps to reduce the saltiness of the stock so that the soup doesn't end up too salty.
- If you have some ham stock – or even a well-flavoured vegetable stock – use this instead of the ham hock for a thriftier soup. Add the soaked split peas, a finely chopped onion, carrot, celery stick and the peppercorns and herbs listed above, and simmer until soft. Serve with a sprinkling of smoked paprika.
- Some hocks are meatier than others: if you're lucky you'll have some succulent ham left over for sandwiches or a pasta bake.

Put the ham hock in a large bowl, add cold water to cover and leave to soak for 3 hours.

Put the split peas in a separate bowl, add cold water to cover and leave to soak for 2 hours.

Drain the hock, then put it in a large, deep saucepan. Add the onion, carrots, celery, peppercorns and herbs, add cold water to cover and bring slowly to the boil. Reduce the heat, cover and simmer gently for 2 hours or until the ham is very tender. You may need to top up the water level to keep the hock covered.

Use a slotted spoon to lift the ham hock out of the stock and set aside. Strain the stock into a large bowl; there should be about 1.5 litres (2½ pints) – if necessary, add some boiling water. Return the stock to the rinsed-out pan.

Drain and rinse the split peas, add to the stock, bring to the boil and boil rapidly for 10 minutes, then cover and simmer gently for 1 hour or until the split peas are soft.

When the hock is cool enough to handle, cut all the meat off the bone, shred it and set it aside.

Briefly blitz the split pea soup with a stick blender: it shouldn't be completely smooth. Taste and season with pepper and a little salt, if needed (the ham stock may be salty enough). Reheat if needed, then serve in bowls, adding a small pile of shredded ham to the centre of each bowl.

Scotch Broth

Serves   **4**
Prep   **20 mins, plus soaking**
Cook   **about 2 hours**

This is a substantial bowl of pulses, grains and veg and it's traditionally made with mutton, although sometimes with beef. While the lamb in this recipe gives it an excellent flavour, the soup can be made with a meat stock to provide flavour without the meat.

100g (3½oz) yellow or green split peas

500g (1lb 2oz) scrag end or neck of lamb on the bone, cut into roughly 3cm (1¼in) pieces

100g (3½oz) pearl barley

2 onions, diced

4 carrots, diced

2 small turnips, diced, or a piece of swede, about 150g (5½oz)

3 tbsp chopped fresh parsley

Salt and pepper

Soak the split peas in cold water for 2 hours. Drain in a sieve and rinse under cold water, then put them into a large saucepan.

Add the lamb, a little salt and pepper and 1.2 litres (2 pints) water, and bring just to the boil over a medium-high heat. Skim off any scum and then add the pearl barley. Bring back to the boil, then reduce the heat, cover and simmer very gently for 1 hour.

Add the vegetables and simmer for another 40 minutes, or until the split peas, barley and vegetables are soft.

Using a slotted spoon, lift out the lamb. When cool enough to handle, take all the meat off the bones and return it to the broth. Season to taste, add the parsley and reheat: this should be served very hot.

Tips

- This is a perfect dish to make after you have had a roast leg or shoulder of lamb: use the bone, ideally with a bit of meat clinging to it, instead of the neck specified. The thriftiest recipes for Scotch broth use no meat at all – just lamb or mutton stock with the barley, pulses and vegetables.
- You could even make a vegan version, using a well-flavoured vegetable stock.
- Instead of neck of lamb you can use 2 lamb shanks (if possible, ask your butcher to chop them into 2 or 3 pieces), but they will need longer simmering to become fall-off-the-bone tender.

Meal in a Bowl

Our Iron Age ancestors found that when meat was simmered in their cooking pot it became more tender than when roasted over direct heat. This made it more digestible and therefore provided more energy. Soups and stews (known in medieval times as 'pottage' – 'food cooked in a pot') have always been infinitely varied, reflecting the ingredients found in different parts of the world. If meat, game or poultry was available – or affordable – it would often go into the pot along with vegetables, pulses or grains. One such dish with a long history is the Welsh cawl, a soup-stew based on lamb or beef simmered with leeks, cabbage and root vegetables – but it contains no grains, because of the lack of arable land in Wales. Some of the classic French 'peasant' soups, with regional and seasonal variations throughout France, date back even further. *Potée*, for example, is a vegetable soup-stew (where cabbage usually plays an important part) with pork in various forms (bacon, ham, sausage, head, ears, tail). *Pot-au-feu* ('pot on the fire') is similar but often based on beef, and in south-west France you'll find *garbure*, which might include goose or duck confit as well as pork. Some of these soups make even more of a meal, being served in two courses: first the broth (which may be ladled onto a sop of bread) and then the meat and vegetables arranged on plates as the main course.

It's the sop of bread used to soak up the liquid (as in the term 'sopping wet') that gave its name (*soupe*) to these rustic French dishes, and to similar dishes throughout Europe, from Italy's *zuppa* to Sweden's *soppa*. In England the terms 'pottage' and 'broth' had been used for centuries, but after the Restoration of Charles II in 1660 there was a fashion for all things French, and the word 'soup' came into general use.

Of course, many of the soups in this book can be enjoyed as a meal in a bowl, especially those made with pulses, pasta or grains, but in this chapter it's the chicken or meat that is the star. Chicken is supremely versatile and is the base of diverse soups around the world. Some are substantial soup-stews, whereas others are lighter broths that rely on good chicken stock – which can, of course, be made from leftover roast chicken. Soup is a perfect way to make a small amount of meat or chicken go a lot further, as you will discover in this chapter.

Cream of Chicken and Tarragon Soup

Serves **4**
Prep **20 mins**
Cook **30 mins**

GF Gluten-free

Fragrant and comforting, as chicken soup should be, this was created by the National Trust chefs. The crispy chicken skin is optional, but it adds a contrasting texture to this creamy soup.

2 boneless chicken thighs with skin

1 tbsp vegetable oil

1 large onion, finely chopped

1 celery stick, finely chopped

1 leek, white part only, finely chopped

1 carrot, finely chopped

850ml (1½ pints) chicken stock

2 tbsp finely chopped fresh tarragon

2 tbsp cornflour

6 tbsp milk

4 tbsp double cream

Salt and pepper

Remove the chicken skin and set it aside. Dice the chicken.

Heat the oil in a large saucepan over a medium heat, add the onion, celery and a pinch of salt, and cook for 5 minutes or until beginning to soften.

Add the diced chicken and fry for 5 minutes, stirring until lightly browned. Add the leek and carrot and stir well. Pour in the stock, add half the tarragon, season with a little salt and pepper and bring to the boil, then reduce the heat, cover and simmer for 10–15 minutes until the chicken is cooked through.

Meanwhile, make the crispy chicken skin (see below), if you like.

Put the cornflour in a small bowl, add half the milk and mix to a smooth paste. Pour into the saucepan, stirring all the time, then add the remaining milk and bring back to the boil. Reduce the heat and simmer for 5 minutes or until thickened, stirring.

Stir in the cream and the remaining tarragon, then taste and adjust the seasoning. Serve in bowls, with crispy chicken skin broken over the top.

Crispy Chicken Skin

Ask your butcher to set aside some chicken skin for you. It's worth getting extra skin if you can, as it shrinks considerably during cooking.

Preheat the oven to 200°C/180°C fan/gas 6 and line a baking sheet with baking paper. Lay the chicken skin on a board, skin-side down, and use a small sharp knife to scrape off as much fat as you can. Place, skin-side down, on the lined baking sheet, stretching the skins flat. Sprinkle with a pinch of salt. Cover the skins with another sheet of baking paper, then another baking sheet, and cook in the oven for 15 minutes or until golden brown. Place the skins on a plate lined with kitchen paper to drain and crisp up.

Thai-Style Chicken and Coconut Soup

Serves **4**
Prep **15 mins**
Cook **15 mins**

GF Gluten-free

Inspired by the Thai soup *tom kha gai*, the distinguishing flavour here is galangal, or *kha*. Formerly known as galingale, and related to ginger, galangal was widely used in wealthy households throughout the Middle Ages but had fallen out of fashion by the 17th century. This version includes green beans and green cabbage to make a more substantial soup.

500ml (18fl oz) chicken stock

400ml (14fl oz) full-fat coconut milk

4cm (1½in) piece galangal, peeled and sliced or chopped into 3 or 4 pieces

2 lemongrass stalks, outer layer removed, bruised

4 kaffir (makrut) lime leaves, torn in half

1–2 fresh red chillies, to taste, deseeded and thinly sliced

1 tsp soft brown sugar

2 large or 3 small skinless, boneless chicken thighs, about 300g (10½oz), sliced

170g (6oz) green beans, cut into 3cm (1¼in) lengths

100g (3½oz) green cabbage, shredded

6 spring onions, thinly sliced

1–2 tbsp Thai fish sauce, to taste

Juice of 1–2 limes, to taste

Small handful of fresh coriander

Salt

Put the stock and coconut milk in a large saucepan over a low heat, add the galangal, lemongrass, lime leaves, chillies, sugar and a pinch of salt, and slowly bring to the boil.

Add the chicken and simmer for 5 minutes. Add the beans and cabbage, bring back to the boil, then reduce the heat and simmer for 3 minutes.

Stir in the spring onions, 1 tablespoon of the fish sauce and 1 tablespoon of the lime juice. Taste and add more fish sauce or lime juice to balance the flavours. Serve.

Tips

- Instead of green beans, use runner beans, stringed and cut into 2cm (¾in) slices, sugar snap peas or mangetout. You could also add 100g (3½oz) sliced fresh mushrooms (any kind: white, shiitake, oyster).
- Fresh galangal, kaffir lime leaves and lemongrass are available from some supermarkets and Asian shops. If you can't find them fresh, you might find them frozen. Dried galangal and lime leaves (but not lemongrass) would work too. As an alternative to galangal you could use fresh ginger. These ingredients are not eaten, though they are traditionally left in the soup: I prefer to fish them out before serving.

Chicken Broth Three Ways

Here are three recipes inspired by Italian methods of using a good stock as the basis of simple yet elegant soups. Start with a well-flavoured Chicken Stock (page 146): make it from scratch or use a leftover roast chicken carcass.

Alphabet Soup

Serves	4
Prep	5 mins
Cook	10 mins

1 litre (1¾ pints) chicken stock (page 146)

100g (3½oz) alphabet pasta

170g (6oz) cooked chicken, shredded (optional)

Grated Parmesan, to serve (optional)

This is based on the Italian *pastina in brodo*. Children love alphabet pasta, but you can use any tiny pasta shapes such as stars or orzo. It's served as a light first course and is also soothing if you're feeling a bit under the weather. Cooking the pasta separately keeps the broth clear, or you can boil it in the broth if you prefer.

Bring the stock just to the boil in a saucepan.

Meanwhile, in a separate pan of boiling water, cook the pasta until it is almost tender (about 5 minutes). Drain and add to the stock, along with the chicken, if using, and simmer for a further 5 minutes to heat the chicken through. Serve hot – sprinkle with a little grated Parmesan, if you like.

Egg Drop Soup

Serves	4
Prep	5 mins
Cook	5 mins

1 litre (1¾ pints) chicken stock

4 eggs, at room temperature

4 tbsp finely grated Parmesan

Freshly grated nutmeg or finely grated zest of ½–1 lemon, to taste

2 tbsp finely chopped fresh parsley

Salt and pepper

In Italian, *stracciatelle* are 'little rags', and in this soup they're made from eggs. In Italy, *stracciatella* soup appears everywhere from smart restaurants to thrifty kitchens. It's also a nourishing soup for convalescents.

Bring the stock to the boil in a saucepan.

In a bowl, using a large fork, beat the eggs with the Parmesan, nutmeg or lemon zest and a good pinch of salt. Stir in the parsley.

When the stock is boiling steadily, slowly pour in the egg mixture, stirring so that the egg forms little clumps. Reduce the heat and simmer for 1 minute, still stirring, then serve immediately.

Serves   **4**
Prep   **15 mins**
Cook   **10 mins**

200g (7oz) cooked chicken

50g (1¾oz) fresh breadcrumbs

2 tbsp freshly grated Parmesan

2 tbsp finely chopped fresh parsley, sage or basil

2 eggs, beaten

1.2 litres (2 pints) chicken stock

Salt and pepper

Chicken Broth with Chicken Dumplings

The little dumplings in this recipe are easy to make from leftover cooked chicken and breadcrumbs.

Put the chicken in a food processor or mini chopper and mince finely. Transfer to a bowl. Add the breadcrumbs, Parmesan, herbs, salt and pepper and mix well. Stir in the beaten eggs to make a firm mixture. Run your hands under the cold tap and then shape the mixture into hazelnut-sized balls.

To serve, bring the stock to a simmer in a large saucepan, add the dumplings and simmer gently for 5–8 minutes until piping hot, then serve.

Tips

- Add sliced mushrooms, baby spinach leaves, courgettes cut into matchsticks, or shredded green cabbage to the broth along with the dumplings.
- If you like, garnish with crispy fried sage leaves (page 53).

Serves **4**
Prep **20 mins**
Cook **2 hours**

GF Gluten-free

Chicken, Vegetable and Rice Noodle Broth

Transform leftover roast chicken into this gently spiced, colourful chicken soup, inspired by a recipe from the National Trust chefs. The broth tastes even better when made with leftover roast duck. It's also a fun way to use up small amounts of vegetables that might otherwise be wasted. Serve with chopsticks to help you slurp up the noodles.

50g (1¾oz) mangetout, sliced lengthways

50g (1¾oz) broccoli, thinly sliced

50g (1¾oz) frozen peas

50g (1¾oz) frozen sweetcorn

85g (3oz) dried fine rice noodles (vermicelli)

½ a red pepper, deseeded and thinly sliced

100g (3½oz) beansprouts, rinsed in cold water, drained

200g (7oz) cooked chicken, shredded

1 tbsp soy sauce, or to taste

2 tbsp chopped fresh coriander (optional)

Salt and pepper

Spiced broth

1 roast chicken carcass, broken into small pieces

1 onion, halved

1 large carrot, cut into chunks

1 celery stick, roughly chopped

2 star anise

2 garlic cloves, lightly crushed

a few slices of fresh ginger

1 tsp coriander seeds, lightly crushed (optional)

A few fresh coriander stalks (optional)

To make the broth, put the chicken carcass in a large saucepan. Add the onion, carrot, celery, star anise, garlic, ginger, coriander seeds and coriander stalks, if using. Add a pinch of salt and cold water to just cover the bones, about 1.2 litres (2 pints), and bring to the boil. Reduce the heat so that the liquid simmers very gently, with the pan partly covered, for 2 hours. Strain into a clean pan. You should have about 850ml (1½ pints): if there's much more, bring it back to the boil and simmer to reduce the liquid.

When the broth is almost ready, steam the mangetout, broccoli, peas and sweetcorn for 3 minutes. Plunge into cold water to cool quickly, then drain well and put in a mixing bowl.

Cook the rice noodles or soak in boiling water, according to the packet instructions. Drain in a colander.

Add the red pepper, beansprouts and noodles to the steamed vegetables and mix together.

Add the shredded chicken to the broth along with the soy sauce, and bring slowly back to the boil. Taste and adjust the seasoning, adding more soy sauce if needed.

Divide the noodle mix between four serving bowls, ladle over the hot broth, sprinkle with the chopped coriander, if you like, and serve immediately.

Tips

- You can make the broth up to one day ahead; strain it into a bowl, cover and chill. To use, remove any excess fat from the top, pour into a saucepan, add the chicken and soy sauce, and bring slowly to the boil, as above.
- You can make the broth in a pressure cooker in 40 minutes: follow the manufacturer's instructions – you will need less liquid, as it takes less time to extract the flavour from the chicken.
- Instead of rice noodles you could use soba noodles, which are made from buckwheat and are naturally gluten-free (but check the pack). If you don't need this soup to be gluten-free, you could use udon noodles instead.
- Swap any of the vegetables in the list with pak choi or Chinese leaves, sliced into 1cm (½in) thick ribbons; sliced mushrooms (button, oyster or shiitake), or carrots or courgettes, cut into matchsticks and added with the red pepper.
- If you're making this for children, cut the vegetables (and the noodles if you wish) into spoon-sized pieces to make it easier to eat.
- If you don't have fresh coriander, garnish with spring onions, thinly sliced at an angle.

Moroccan-Style Vegetable and Chicken Soup

Serves **4**
Prep **20 mins**
Cook **30–35 mins**

GF Gluten-free

Aromatic with cumin and cinnamon, this Moroccan-inspired soup-stew includes chickpeas, tomatoes and apricots for a healthy and satisfying bowlful. Developed by the National Trust chefs, it's sure to warm you up on a chilly day. Serve with crusty bread or warmed flatbreads.

1 tbsp olive oil

1 large onion, chopped

1 celery stick, diced

2 large carrots, diced

2 garlic cloves, finely chopped

1 heaped tsp ground cumin

1 tsp ground cinnamon

½ tsp ground turmeric

1 tbsp harissa

1½ tbsp tomato purée

2 large or 3 small skinless, boneless chicken thighs, about 300g (10½oz), sliced

400g (14oz) tin chickpeas, drained and rinsed

200g (7oz) tinned chopped tomatoes

400ml (14fl oz) chicken stock

50g (1¾oz) dried ready-to-eat apricots, chopped

3 tbsp chopped fresh flat-leaf parsley

Salt and pepper

Heat the oil in a large saucepan over a medium-high heat, add the onion, celery, carrots and a pinch of salt, and cook for 10 minutes or until beginning to soften.

Add the garlic, spices, harissa and tomato purée, and cook, stirring, for 2 minutes. Push the spicy vegetable mixture to the side of the pan and add the chicken; season with a little salt and pepper, and cook for 5–6 minutes until lightly browned all over.

Add the chickpeas, tomatoes and stock. Bring to the boil and then reduce the heat, partly cover and simmer for 10–15 minutes until the chicken is cooked through.

Stir in the apricots and most of the parsley, then taste and adjust the seasoning. Ladle into bowls and top with the remaining parsley.

Greek-Style Chicken Soup

Serves **4**
Prep **10 mins**
Cook **30–45 mins**

In Greek cooking, *avgolemono* is a silky egg and lemon sauce that is served with fish, chicken or meat dishes and is also used to thicken soups. *Avgolemono* soup is usually based on chicken stock, or sometimes fish stock. Rice, or the grain-like pasta called orzo, adds gentle texture to the soup: for a more substantial soup, use more rice or orzo.

1 litre (1¾ pints) chicken stock

2 skinless chicken breasts or 3 skinless thighs on the bone

50g (1¾oz) long grain rice or orzo

2 eggs, at room temperature

Juice of 1 large lemon

1 tbsp finely chopped parsley or dill

½ lemon, very thinly sliced, to garnish (optional)

Salt and pepper

Put the stock and chicken in a large saucepan over a medium-high heat. Bring just to the boil, then turn down the heat and simmer for 15–25 minutes until the chicken is cooked through. Lift the chicken out of the stock and set aside.

Taste the stock and season with salt and pepper. Bring back to the boil, add the rice and cook for 10–15 minutes until tender; orzo will take slightly less time to cook.

Meanwhile, shred the chicken, removing the bones. Divide the meat among four soup plates.

Break the eggs into a bowl, add the lemon juice and whisk until frothy. Remove the pan of stock from the heat. Gradually add a ladleful of the hot stock to the egg mixture, whisking well, then another ladleful: the egg mixture should be warm and beginning to thicken. Whisk the mixture into the pan of stock until it thickens slightly. You may need to put the pan back over a low heat to thicken the soup, but don't let the soup boil or the eggs will curdle.

Ladle the soup over the chicken and serve immediately, lightly sprinkled with parsley or dill. If you like, add a few slices of lemon to garnish.

Boxing Day Soup

Serves   **4–6**
Prep   **20 mins**
Cook   **about 2½ hours**

There's no rule that says you have to eat turkey (pie, curry, sandwiches) on each of the 12 days of Christmas. Instead, you could strip off the meat and freeze it, separating the dark meat from the white, to enjoy over the next two or three months. Use the carcass as the basis for this tasty, spicy soup, to which you can add any other festive leftovers, from roasted roots to pigs in blankets.

1 roasted turkey carcass, including skin, broken into pieces, plus some leftover roast turkey, chopped or shredded

3 onions: 2 halved, 1 chopped

3 carrots, roughly chopped

2 celery sticks, roughly chopped

3 garlic cloves: 2 whole, 1 chopped

2 bay leaves

10 peppercorns

1 tbsp vegetable oil, or fat saved from roasting the turkey

4 bacon rashers, chopped, or 80g (2¾oz) bacon lardons

1–2 tsp smoked paprika, to taste

Roast potatoes, parsnips, carrots or other roasted roots, chopped

Cooked pigs in blankets, chopped

400g (14oz) tin chopped tomatoes or passata

Leftover cooked sprouts or other green vegetables, sliced

Salt and pepper

Cranberry sauce or grated cheese, to serve (optional)

Put the turkey bones into a large saucepan or stockpot and add cold water to cover, about 2 litres (3½ pints). Add the halved onions, carrots, celery, whole garlic, bay leaves, peppercorns and a good pinch of salt, then cover with a lid and bring just to the boil. Skim off the foam and reduce the heat so that the liquid simmers gently, with the pan partly covered, for 2 or preferably 3 hours. Leave to cool slightly, then ladle the liquid through a sieve into a bowl (using a ladle prevents splashing). When you have ladled out most of the liquid, tip the bones and vegetables into the sieve to allow them to drain.

Heat the oil in a large saucepan over a medium heat, add the chopped onion and garlic, the bacon and a pinch of salt, and cook until the onion has softened. Add the paprika and stir, then add the root vegetables, chopped turkey and pigs in blankets, the tomatoes and about 1 litre (1¾ pints) of the turkey stock. Bring to the boil, reduce the heat and simmer for 5–10 minutes.

Add the cooked vegetables and some more stock, if needed, to adjust the consistency to your liking, and simmer for a few more minutes to heat through. Season to taste and serve immediately, topped with a spoonful of cranberry sauce or some grated cheese, if you like.

Tips

- You can make turkey stock in a pressure cooker in about 40 minutes: follow the manufacturer's instructions – you will need less liquid as it takes less time to extract the flavour from the carcass.

- This soup would work just as well with chicken.

- If you don't have any leftover cooked green vegetables, you could boil some fresh ones while the soup is simmering, then add as above.

Pheasant, Puy Lentil and Cumin Soup

Serves **4**
Prep **20 mins**
Cook **3–4 hours**

GF Gluten-free

If you've roasted some game birds – pheasant, partridge, guinea fowl, quail or pigeon – make another meal out of the carcasses with this wholesome autumn and winter soup.

Game stock

2 leftover roast pheasant or guinea fowl carcasses, or 4 or more carcasses of smaller birds

1 onion, halved

1 large carrot, halved

2 celery sticks, roughly chopped

1 leek, green top only, roughly chopped (optional)

2 bay leaves

2 thyme sprigs

4 peppercorns

Pinch of salt

150ml (5fl oz) red wine

Puy lentil soup

1 tbsp vegetable oil

100g (3½oz) smoked streaky bacon, chopped, or bacon lardons or cubed pancetta

1 onion (red or white), finely chopped

1 large carrot, diced

1 celery stick, finely chopped

1 garlic clove, finely chopped

2 tsp ground cumin

2 tbsp tomato purée

170g (6oz) Puy lentils, rinsed

A squeeze of lemon juice, or to taste

Salt and pepper

To serve

2 tbsp Greek-style yogurt

2 tbsp pomegranate molasses, or 3 tbsp good-quality cranberry sauce, sieved

2 tbsp chopped fresh parsley, to serve

Preheat the oven to 200°C/180°C fan/gas 6. Break up or roughly chop the carcasses, pulling off any remaining pieces of meat and setting them aside. Put the bones in a roasting tin and roast for 10–15 minutes until beginning to brown and smell roasty.

Tip the bones into a saucepan and add the onion, carrot, celery, leek (if using), bay leaves, thyme, peppercorns and salt. Pour the red wine into the roasting tin, put over a medium heat and stir to scrape up all the bits that have stuck to the bottom, then add to the pan with the bones. Add water to cover the bones, about 1.2 litres (2 pints), and bring to the boil, then reduce the heat, partly cover the pan, and simmer for 2 or preferably 3 hours; skim off any scum that rises to the surface.

Strain the stock and set aside.

To make the soup, heat the oil in a large saucepan over a medium heat, add the bacon and onion, and cook for 5–10 minutes, stirring occasionally, until softened. Add the carrot, celery and garlic, and cook for a further 5 minutes. Add the cumin and tomato purée, and cook, stirring, for a further 1 minute.

Add the lentils and 800ml (28fl oz) of the stock, then bring to the boil. Reduce the heat, skim, then simmer, partly covered, for 25–40 minutes until the lentils are soft, stirring from time to time.

Blitz half the soup with a stick blender until smooth, then return it to the pan. You might want to adjust the consistency by adding a little more stock or just-boiled water, but don't make it too wet.

Add any reserved meat to the soup and bring back to the boil for 4–5 minutes until piping hot. Add a good squeeze of lemon juice, then taste and adjust the seasoning. Serve topped with a spoonful of yogurt, drizzled with pomegranate molasses or cranberry sauce and sprinkled with chopped parsley.

Tips

- You can mix the birds in this soup, so if you don't have enough to make the soup, keep your roasted leftovers in a sealed bag or container in the freezer for up to 3 months until you have some more.
- You can make the stock up to 3 days ahead and keep it in the fridge; or freeze it. If making a soup using a stock you've prepared in advance, make sure you consume the soup immediately.
- You can use other small green or brown lentils instead of Puy. The cooking time depends on the age and size of the lentils, so be sure to cook them until they are soft and creamy before you blitz them.

Chicken Soup with Matzo Balls

Serves	**4–6**
Prep	**20 mins, plus chilling**
Cook	**2–3½ hours**

Hailed as a miraculous cure-all, the traditional chicken soup is simmered for at least 3 hours, which makes it a good source of collagen – and some studies suggest that this has various health benefits. The jury is still out, but there's no doubt that it can make you feel better. This version is just as comforting but slightly quicker to make, keeping the flavour in the chicken and carrots. In Jewish cuisine, matzo balls are light fluffy dumplings, traditionally cooked separately from the soup.

1 small chicken, cut into 4 pieces, or 2–3 plump legs

6 carrots, cut into 2cm (¾in) pieces

2 onions, roughly chopped

2 celery sticks, roughly chopped

Handful of fresh parsley stalks and leaves

1 tsp sea salt flakes

10 black peppercorns

Salt and pepper

Chopped fresh dill, to serve

Matzo balls

2 large eggs

60g (2¼oz) medium matzo meal

½ tsp salt

2 tbsp melted chicken fat or vegetable oil

2 tbsp chicken stock or water

Put the chicken in a large saucepan, add cold water to cover it, about 1.7 litres (3 pints), and slowly bring to the boil. Carefully skim off the scum: you will need to do this several times to ensure your chicken soup is clear and golden. Leave to simmer for 25 minutes. Add the carrots, onions, celery, parsley, salt and peppercorns, topping up with more cold water to cover if needed. Bring back to the boil, then reduce the heat, partly cover the pan and leave to simmer gently for 1–1½ hours until the chicken is cooked through.

Meanwhile, to make the matzo balls, break the eggs into a bowl and whisk well with a fork. Add the matzo meal, salt, chicken fat and stock, and whisk with the fork to make a paste. Cover and chill for at least 30 minutes or overnight.

Place a colander over a large bowl and ladle the hot liquid into the colander (using a ladle prevents splashing). When you have ladled out most of the liquid, tip the chicken and vegetables into the colander and leave to drip through. Pick the chicken and carrots out of the colander and set aside. At this stage, cool the soup quickly, then cover and place it in the fridge overnight (keeping the chicken and carrots in a separate covered container). The next day you'll be able to lift off the fat easily (keep it in the fridge for up to a month and use it for frying onions, roasting potatoes, or making matzo balls another time).

To make the matzo balls, wet your hands and take small pieces of the matzo mixture, gently shaping it into small balls about 2cm (¾in) in diameter – you should get 20–24 balls. Put them on a plate until you have used all the mixture. Bring a large pan of salted water to the boil. Drop the balls into the water, cover the pan and simmer for 30–40 minutes: they will swell up and become light and fluffy.

Meanwhile, remove the chicken meat from the bones and cut into spoon-sized pieces. Skim some of the fat off the top of the soup, then put the soup into a large saucepan, add the carrots and reheat until simmering. Taste and season generously, then add the chicken.

Using a slotted spoon, lift the matzo balls out of their poaching water and add to the soup. Ladle the soup into warmed bowls and serve immediately, sprinkled with dill.

Tips

- Don't be too fussy about removing all the chicken fat from the soup: a little fat adds flavour and richness.
- Chicken fat adds flavour to the matzo balls.
- Instead of small matzo balls, you could make 8–12 larger ones; they will take roughly the same time to cook.
- The matzo balls are simmered in water and not in the soup because they absorb a lot of liquid and would make the soup cloudy.

Chicken, Peanut and Pumpkin Soup

Serves **4–6**
Prep **20 mins**
Cook **35 mins**

GF Gluten-free

Inspired by West African groundnut stew, this hearty meal in a bowl makes a small amount of chicken go a long way – even further if you add rice and greens (see Tip). It's perfect for an autumn day, when pumpkins and squash are plentiful.

1 tbsp vegetable oil (use groundnut oil if you have it)

3 boneless chicken thighs

1 large onion, finely chopped

1 green pepper, deseeded and diced

2 garlic cloves, finely chopped

2.5cm (1in) piece fresh ginger, peeled and grated

1 tsp ground cumin

½–1 red chilli, to taste, deseeded and finely chopped, or a pinch of dried chilli flakes

500g (1lb 2oz) pumpkin or butternut squash, peeled and cut into 2cm (¾in) dice

400ml (14fl oz) chicken stock

400g (14oz) tin chopped tomatoes

4 tbsp (80g/2¾oz) unsweetened peanut butter

Squeeze of lemon or lime juice, to taste

Salt and pepper

Heat the oil in a large saucepan over a medium heat, add the chicken thighs, skin-side down, and fry until well browned, then turn and brown on the other side. Remove from the pan and set aside.

Add the onion and green pepper to the pan, along with the garlic, ginger, cumin, chilli and a pinch of salt, and cook for 7–8 minutes until beginning to soften.

Meanwhile, dice the chicken.

Add the pumpkin to the pan and stir to coat it in the spicy mixture. Return the chicken to the pan, add the stock and tomatoes, then season with salt and pepper. Bring to the boil, then reduce the heat, partly cover the pan and simmer for 15–25 minutes until the pumpkin is tender.

In a small bowl, mix the peanut butter with a ladleful or two of the hot liquid until evenly blended, then mix it into the soup. Bring back to a simmer, then taste and adjust the seasoning, adding a squeeze of lemon or lime juice if needed. If you prefer a slightly thicker soup, you can ladle out some of the soup and blitz it with a stick blender until smooth, then return it to the pan. Reheat if needed. Ladle into bowls and serve hot.

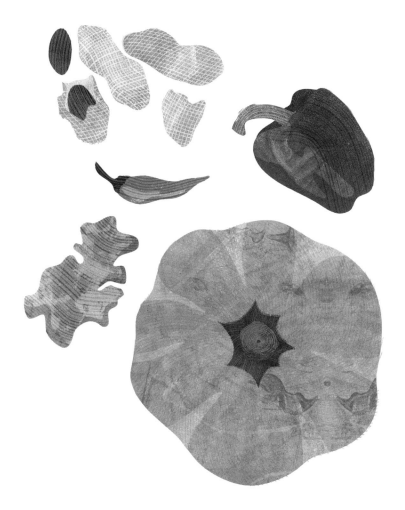

Tips

- Vegetarians and vegans can happily leave out the chicken and replace the stock with vegetable stock.
- Use crunchy or smooth peanut butter – whichever you have in your cupboard.
- If you like, add 50g (1¾oz) uncooked rice when you add the pumpkin. You could also add a handful of spinach or chopped green cabbage towards the end of the cooking time.

Cock-a-Leekie Soup

Serves **4–6**
Prep **20 mins**
Cook **50 mins**

 Gluten-free

Traditionally, this soup was made with an old cockerel or boiling fowl, and sometimes included beef shin for a full-flavoured broth. Modern chickens don't need such long simmering, however, so aim to start with a good, well-flavoured stock. According to the recipe in the *Cook and Housewife's Manual* (1826), written under the pseudonym Meg Dods, 'The soup must be very thick of leeks', so don't hold back. Old-style dried prunes needed soaking or simmering, but these days it's easier to buy ready-to-eat prunes which just need warming through. Some cooks reject the prunes, but I like their slightly spicy tang and black colour.

6 plump leeks

3 plump chicken legs, skin on

1 litre (1¾ pints) well-flavoured chicken stock

1 bouquet garni (see Tip)

10 ready-to-eat prunes, halved

4 tbsp chopped fresh parsley

Salt and pepper

Chop off (and discard or save for stock) the coarse dark green outer leaves at the top of the leeks. Wash the leeks and cut into 4cm (1½in) lengths.

Put the chicken in a large saucepan, add the stock, bouquet garni and a pinch of salt, and bring to the boil. Skim off any scum, then add half the leeks and reduce the heat to a simmer. Partly cover the pan and simmer for 35–40 minutes until the chicken is cooked through.

Remove the chicken and bouquet garni from the soup. Add the remaining leeks, season with salt and pepper and bring the soup back to the boil for 5–10 minutes until the leeks are tender, adding the prunes and parsley for the last few minutes.

Meanwhile, shred the chicken meat, discarding the bones. Divide the chicken among the warmed soup plates, then ladle the soup on top and serve hot.

Tips

- To make a bouquet garni, make a little cylinder of a piece of leek about 7cm (2¾in) long, a piece of celery, a large bay leaf, some parsley stalks and a thyme sprig, and tie firmly with plenty of kitchen string, leaving the end of the string to help you remove the herbs. (Alternatively, put the herbs in a small piece of muslin and tie up the top like a sack, again leaving a long piece of string.)
- You could use a small whole chicken, jointed, instead of chicken legs.

Chicken, Chorizo and Butter Beans

Serves **4**
Prep **20 mins**
Cook **35 mins**

GF Gluten-free

Butter beans and juicy red peppers complement plump chorizo and chicken in this soup. To complete the feast, serve with crusty bread and rocket.

1 tsp olive oil

170g (6oz) cooking chorizo, roughly chopped

1 large onion, finely sliced

2 large garlic cloves, finely sliced

2 large or 3 small skinless, boneless chicken thighs, about 300g (10½oz), sliced

400g (14oz) tin butter beans, drained and rinsed

200g (7oz) roasted red peppers (from a jar), or 2 roasted and skinned red peppers (see Tip), sliced

500ml (18fl oz) chicken stock

Salt and pepper

Heat the oil in a large saucepan over a medium heat, add the chorizo and fry for 3–4 minutes until it releases its oil. Using a slotted spoon, lift it out of the pan and set aside.

Add the onion, garlic and a pinch of salt, and cook for 7–8 minutes until beginning to soften. Add the chicken and cook for 5–6 minutes until lightly browned all over.

Add the butter beans and peppers and return the chorizo to the pan; stir well. Pour in the stock and season with salt and pepper. Bring to the boil, then reduce the heat, partly cover and simmer for 10–15 minutes until the chicken is cooked through.

Taste and adjust the seasoning. Ladle into bowls and serve hot.

Tips

• To roast red peppers: preheat the grill to hot. Halve and deseed the peppers. Grill, skin-side up, until the skin blackens, then place on a plate, cover with a bowl and leave to cool: the skin should now peel off easily.

• For big appetites, add another diced chicken thigh.

105

Moroccan-Style Lamb, Lentil and Chickpea Soup

Serves **6**
Prep **15 mins**
Cook **1½ hours**

During the month of Ramadan – which is different each year because it's based on the lunar calendar – Muslims fast from sunrise to sunset. In Morocco it's traditional to break the fast with a bowl of *harira*, a fragrant and nutritious soup of chickpeas, lentils and fresh herbs. It's typically made with lamb, although some families use chicken – or you can leave out the meat altogether, for a vegan *harira*.

1 tbsp olive oil

400g (14oz) boneless lamb neck fillet or shoulder, cut into 1cm (½in) pieces

1 large onion, finely chopped

1 celery stick, diced

2 garlic cloves, finely chopped

1 tsp ground cumin

½ tsp ground cinnamon

½ tsp ground ginger

½ tsp ground turmeric

¼ tsp freshly ground black pepper

1 tsp harissa

Pinch of saffron threads, soaked in 2 tbsp hot water

1 litre (1¾ pints) hot chicken or vegetable stock

100g (3½oz) green or brown lentils, rinsed

400g (14oz) tin chopped tomatoes

400g (14oz) tin chickpeas, drained and rinsed

1 tbsp plain flour

100g (3½oz) vermicelli pasta (optional), crushed into small pieces

4 tbsp chopped fresh coriander

4 tbsp chopped fresh parsley

Salt

Heat the oil in a large saucepan over a medium-high heat, add the lamb and fry for 5–10 minutes until lightly browned all over. Remove from the pan and set aside.

Reduce the heat slightly, add the onion and celery and a pinch of salt, and cook for 5–8 minutes until softened.

Add the garlic, spices, harissa and saffron, and cook, stirring, for 2 minutes.

Add the stock and lentils, and bring to the boil for 10 minutes. Return the lamb, with any resting juices, to the pan, add the tomatoes, return to the boil, then reduce the heat, cover and simmer gently for 50 minutes until the lamb and lentils are tender.

Add the chickpeas and simmer for 10–15 minutes.

In a small bowl, mix the flour with 2 tablespoons of the hot broth, stirring well to avoid lumps, then stir it into the soup and simmer for a further 10 minutes. If using vermicelli, add it when you add the flour.

Stir in most of the coriander and parsley, then taste and adjust the seasoning. Ladle into bowls and top with the remaining herbs.

Tips

- This is best made the day before you want to serve it. If making ahead, don't add the vermicelli. About 10 minutes before you are ready to serve, bring the soup back to the boil and add the vermicelli.
- To make a vegan *harira*, leave out the meat.
- Although you don't need to soak lentils before cooking, I find that leaving them in their rinsing water for 15 minutes before draining helps them to cook more evenly.

Goulash Soup

Serves **4–6**
Prep **15 mins**
Cook **about
2¾ hours**

 Gluten-free

This traditional Hungarian soup-stew derives its name from *gulyás*, meaning 'herdsman'. It is made from tougher cuts of beef, which enrich the liquid as they cook slowly. Goulash assumed its current identity some 500 years ago, when peppers were introduced to Europe: it uses both fresh peppers and paprika, made from a type of red pepper that is usually mild with a full flavour.

2 tbsp vegetable oil or lard

750g (1lb 10oz) braising steak, cut into 2cm (¾in) cubes

2 large onions, chopped

800ml (28fl oz) beef or vegetable stock

1 red pepper, deseeded and sliced

1 green pepper, deseeded and sliced

1 tbsp tomato purée

2 garlic cloves, sliced

1 tsp caraway seeds, crushed

2 tbsp mild paprika, plus extra to serve

1 tsp smoked paprika

1 bay leaf

400g (14oz) tin cherry tomatoes or chopped tomatoes

½ tsp sugar

340g (12oz) potatoes, cut into 1.5cm (⅝in) chunks

Salt and pepper

To serve

4 tbsp soured cream

2 tbsp chopped fresh parsley

Heat half the oil in a large saucepan over a high heat. Add the meat, in batches, and fry until browned all over, then remove with a slotted spoon and set aside on a plate.

Add the remaining oil to the pan and cook the onions for 5–6 minutes until softened, stirring frequently. Add a splash of the stock if they begin to stick to the pan.

Add the peppers and tomato purée and cook for 5 minutes, stirring frequently. Add the garlic, caraway seeds and both types of paprika. Season well with salt and pepper, and cook, stirring, for a further 1 minute.

Return the beef to the pan and add the stock, bay leaf, tomatoes and sugar. Stir well, cover the pan and simmer over a low heat for 1½–2 hours or until the beef is tender.

Add the potatoes, return to the boil, then reduce the heat, cover and simmer for a further 20–30 minutes or until they are tender.

Taste and adjust the seasoning. Serve with a spoonful of soured cream sprinkled with paprika and chopped parsley.

Tips

- You can make the goulash the day before you want to serve it: the beef will become even more tender.
- Use beef shin, beef cheek or another cut suitable for slow cooking.
- You can use a pressure cooker to save cooking time for the meat: follow the manufacturer's instructions – you will need to use less liquid for cooking, but you may need to add a little more when you simmer the potatoes on the hob. If you want to add Dumplings (page 155), put them on top of the soup when you add the potatoes.

Fish and Shellfish

The British Isles are surrounded by sea, and laced with lakes and rivers, so the lack of traditional fish soups – Scotland's Cullen Skink (page 125) being a notable exception – is a bit of a mystery; however, that's not to say that coastal dwellers haven't always used fish and shellfish in broths, pottages and soups – whatever they couldn't sell would go into the pot. Mussels, cockles, clams, whelks, winkles and oysters were easy to gather and inexpensive to buy; shrimps, prawns, crabs and lobsters achieved higher prices. The range of sea fish eaten over the centuries would amaze modern fishmongers. Lakes and rivers provided the hugely popular eel (now critically endangered) and salmon, as well as crayfish, pike, perch and many others.

In every part of the world, fish soups and stews have evolved according to local species and easily obtainable ingredients; precise recipes are therefore impossible to pin down since all were dependent on the catch of the day. Unsaleable fish – those that are small, bony or less than perfect – are often full of flavour. They are one of the distinguishing features of the *bouillabaisse* from Marseille in the south of France, but even that famous dish is the subject of much dispute as to the most authentic recipe. The most important thing for any fish soup is that the fish and shellfish must be very fresh.

Throughout history, the battle between humans and fish was one the fishermen were never certain of winning, and nature was able to maintain a balance: there were always plenty more fish in the sea (or river). But by the middle of the 19th century, industrialisation and the ever-increasing demand for food resulted in pollution and over-exploitation of resources. One of the first casualties was England's oyster beds. Oysters had been enjoyed by rich and poor alike for thousands of years, but within a few years they became a rare and expensive luxury. Today, however, oysters, mussels, clams and cockles can be farmed sustainably.

Modern fishing technology developed after the Second World War, combined with bottom trawling (which indiscriminately scoops up marine life, destroys habitats and, we now know, releases vast amounts of carbon dioxide), led to the collapse of the traditional Northwest Atlantic cod fishery off Canada in the early 1990s. It has not recovered. Cod stocks in some other areas have been managed and are sustainable once more. Since cod is a top predator, its losses had impacts all down the food chain, and hence the entire ecosystem. It's not just cod we need to consider: other species are equally under threat from overfishing, while fishing communities have been put in jeopardy as a result of the loss of their traditional livelihood.

The National Trust looks after over 780 miles of coastline and is working closely with other organisations to protect coastal habitats. We can all do our bit to protect marine life by choosing to buy fish and shellfish that have been caught or farmed sustainably: look for the blue tick eco-label of the Marine Stewardship Council. The MSC monitors fisheries around the world to ensure that fish stocks are healthy and give us all the best chance of continuing to enjoy seafood.

Classic Fish Soup

Serves 4
Prep 25 mins
Cook 50 mins

Using the small, bony fish that were historically easy to catch but often difficult to sell, versions of this deeply flavourful soup can be found all along the Mediterranean coast of France. Small fish, heads and all, add both flavour and body. If you can only get larger fish, however, one or two whole fish work well, along with the raw prawns. It's traditionally served with slices of toasted French bread, spicy rouille and grated cheese.

About 1kg (2lb 3oz) small white fish, such as gurnard, sea bass or bream, gutted, scaled, fins removed (see Tip)

2 tbsp olive oil

1 onion, chopped

1 fennel bulb, chopped

2 garlic cloves, chopped

400g (14oz) tin chopped tomatoes

2 tbsp pastis (optional)

150ml (5fl oz) dry white wine

Pinch of dried chilli flakes

5cm (2in) strip of thinly pared orange peel

1 bay leaf

4 thyme sprigs

1 tbsp tomato purée

Good pinch of saffron

About 150g (5½oz) raw prawns in their shells

Salt and pepper

Rouille

1 large red pepper, halved and deseeded

2 garlic cloves, peeled

Pinch of dried chilli flakes

1 tsp tomato purée

30g (1oz) crustless day-old bread, such as French bread or ciabatta, soaked in a little water, then squeezed dry

1 egg yolk

4 tbsp olive oil

To serve

12 small slices of baguette

1 small garlic clove, halved

Grated cheese

—continued overleaf

First, make the rouille. Preheat the grill to hot. Grill the pepper, skin-side up, until the skin blackens, then put on a plate, cover with a bowl and leave to cool: the skin should now peel off easily. Put all the ingredients, except the oil, in a pestle and mortar or a blender. Pound or blitz until smooth, then gradually add the oil until the rouille is thick, like mayonnaise. Season with salt to taste. Set aside.

Rinse the fish and check that no scales remain. Set aside.

Heat the olive oil in a large saucepan over a medium heat, add the onion, fennel and a pinch of salt, and cook for 10 minutes or until softened. Add the garlic and tomatoes and cook for 5 minutes.

Add the pastis, if using, and let it bubble for a minute or two, then add the wine and bring to the boil. Add the chilli flakes, orange peel, bay leaf, thyme, tomato purée and 850ml (1½ pints) water, and bring back to the boil. Put the saffron in a small bowl and add 2 tablespoons of the hot liquid, then stir it into the soup. Add the fish and prawns, cover and simmer very gently for 30 minutes.

Remove the pan from the heat. Carefully pour the soup into a sieve set over a large bowl, then pick out the heads and bones, returning the fish flesh to the sieve. Press the fish and vegetable debris with a ladle or a wooden spoon to extract all the flavour and help to thicken the soup.

Rinse the pan, then return the soup to the pan and season to taste. Reheat gently while you toast the baguette slices on both sides, then rub them with the garlic. Serve the soup with the toast, a small bowl of rouille and a separate bowl of grated cheese, for people to help themselves.

Tips

- Don't use oily fish such as mackerel or sardines: the flavours don't work well in this soup.
- Ask your fishmonger to clean the fish (removing the guts, gills and fins) and descale them. Some fishmongers will give you bones and fish heads for nothing: they will give plenty of flavour to this soup and you could use them instead of some of the fish.
- Cheat's rouille: mix 4 tablespoons mayonnaise with 2 crushed garlic cloves, 1 teaspoon tomato purée and 2–3 teaspoons harissa paste, to taste.
- The soup can be frozen for up to 2 months. Defrost in the fridge and gently reheat until piping hot, stirring regularly, without letting it boil.

Hot and Sour Prawn Broth

Serves **4**
Prep **20 mins**
Cook **15 mins**

 Gluten-free

The soup known in Thailand as *tom yum gung* balances hot, salty and sour flavours, but the authentic version can be lip-numbingly, sweat-inducingly hot, so I've made this version gentler, to keep the flavour of the prawns to the fore. You could serve a separate bowl of Thai roast chilli paste (*nam prik pao*) so that people can stir a little into the soup if they wish – it adds chilli heat and a reddish colour.

1 tbsp vegetable oil

340g (12oz) large raw prawns, shelled and deveined, shells reserved

2 lemongrass stalks, bruised and chopped into 3 or 4 pieces

4 kaffir (makrut) lime leaves, torn into pieces

4cm (1½in) piece galangal or ginger, peeled and sliced or chopped into 3 or 4 pieces

2 fresh red chillies, deseeded and thinly sliced

1 tsp soft brown sugar

150g (5½oz) button mushrooms, sliced

1–2 tbsp Thai fish sauce, or to taste

Juice of 1½–2 limes, to taste

Small handful of fresh coriander leaves

3 spring onions, thinly sliced

Heat the oil in a saucepan over a medium-high heat and fry the prawn shells until they turn pink. Add 1 litre (1¾ pints) water, the lemongrass, lime leaves, galangal and half the sliced chillies, and bring to the boil. Reduce the heat and simmer gently for 10 minutes.

Strain the stock into another pan and bring to a gentle simmer. Add the sugar, prawns and mushrooms, cover and simmer for 2 minutes or until the prawns turn pink. Remove from the heat.

Add 1 tablespoon of the fish sauce and the juice of 1 lime. Taste and add more fish sauce and lime juice if needed to balance the flavours. Serve hot, sprinkled with the reserved red chilli, coriander leaves and spring onions.

Tips

- If you like, replace half the prawns with cubed white fish or sliced squid.
- Add the lime juice just before serving to keep its fresh flavour.
- Leftover lemongrass can be kept in the fridge to keep it fresh, or alternatively it can be frozen. Kaffir lime leaves also freeze well.
- For a more substantial soup, add some sliced pak choi, green beans or peas along with the prawns. You could also add some cooked rice noodles to each bowl before adding the soup.

Crab and Sweetcorn Soup

Serves **4**
Prep **15 mins, or 1 hour if using a whole crab**
Cook **15 mins**

GF Gluten-free

An old favourite of Chinese restaurants, this is simplicity itself to make once your crabmeat is ready – but bear in mind that preparing fresh crab is not a task to leave until the last minute: do it earlier in the day and keep it in the fridge (see Tip). The multi-purpose stock in the Chinese kitchen is traditionally made from a mix of chicken and pork bones, simmered for several hours to concentrate the flavours. A good homemade chicken stock is the thing to aim for here.

- 200g (7oz) cooked white crabmeat, fresh or defrosted frozen
- 1 litre (1¾ pints) well-flavoured chicken stock
- 200g (7oz) frozen sweetcorn
- 2.5cm (1in) fresh ginger, peeled and finely chopped
- 1½ tbsp rice wine or dry sherry
- 1½ tbsp light soy sauce, or to taste
- 1 tsp salt
- 4 tsp cornflour, blended with 4 tsp cold water
- 3 spring onions, thinly sliced
- 1 egg white, lightly beaten (optional)

Check the crabmeat for any little shards of shell, but try not to break it up too much. Set aside.

Bring the stock to the boil in a saucepan. Add the sweetcorn and simmer for 5 minutes. Add the ginger, rice wine, soy sauce, salt and the cornflour mixture, and simmer for 1 minute, then add the crab and spring onions, and simmer for another minute.

If using the egg white, slowly pour it into the simmering soup while stirring quickly with a fork so that the egg forms thin threads. Serve immediately.

Tips

- Use fresh crab for the best flavour. If you come across a fresh cooked crab weighing about 900g (2lb), you can spend a mindful three-quarters of an hour picking out the white meat, which will give you the right amount for this recipe. First, twist off the legs and claws, then separate the main body from the shell. Remove and discard the feathery gills around the body. Using a heavy knife, cut the body in half, then carefully pick out the white meat using the handle of a teaspoon. Using the blunt edge of the knife, crack the claws and legs and remove the meat. Keep the dark meat from the shell for a luxurious sandwich or salad, and freeze the shells to add to fish stock.
- Crab claws, and the legs of spider crabs, full of white meat, are sometimes sold separately. Save the shells and freeze to add to fish stock.
- Frozen sweetcorn has a good flavour, but you could also use two freshly picked corn cobs: use a large knife to slice off the kernels, keeping the knife close to the cob and scraping off as much of the corn and juices as possible. Add the kernels to the boiling stock, then reduce the heat and simmer for 5–10 minutes until tender.
- The egg thread is a traditional way to finish this soup, but skip it if you prefer.

Prawn Bisque

Serves **4**
Prep **25 mins**
Cook **45–50 mins,**
plus cooling

A seafood bisque gets its luxurious flavour from the shells, so this can be a thrifty way of making two meals from your shellfish. You could use most of the prawn flesh in a salad, pasta dish or stir-fry, then freeze the heads, shells and a little of the flesh to make this soup at a later date.

700g (1lb 9oz) raw prawns in shells

40g (1½oz) butter

1 onion, chopped

1 carrot, chopped

1 celery stick, chopped

2 tbsp brandy

150ml (5fl oz) dry white wine

1 tbsp tomato purée

40g (1½oz) long-grain rice

1.2 litres (2 pints) fish stock

1 bouquet garni (see Tip)

Squeeze of lemon juice, or to taste

100ml (3½fl oz) double cream, plus extra (optional) to serve

Salt, ground black pepper and cayenne pepper

Remove the heads and shells from the prawns. Set aside the prawns: you can add some to the bisque later or freeze them to use in another dish.

Melt 30g (1oz) of the butter in a large saucepan over a medium-high heat, add the onion, carrot and celery, and cook for 7–8 minutes until they begin to brown. Add the prawn heads and shells and cook for 3–4 minutes until they turn pink, crushing them with a wooden spoon.

Add the brandy and let it bubble, then add the wine and cook for 1–2 minutes, stirring to dislodge any browned bits from the bottom of the pan. Add the tomato purée and rice and cook, stirring, for 1–2 minutes. Add the fish stock and bouquet garni and bring to the boil, then reduce the heat, cover and simmer gently for 30 minutes.

Leave to cool for 5–10 minutes, then remove the bouquet garni and pour the soup, including the prawn shells, into a food processor and blitz. Pour the soup through a fine sieve into a bowl, pressing the prawn and vegetable debris with a wooden spoon or sturdy spatula to extract the maximum flavour and texture. Be sure to scrape the bottom of the sieve to glean all of the mixture.

If using the prawns, put a small saucepan over a medium-high heat and add the remaining butter. When it foams, add the prawns and stir-fry for 2–3 minutes, until they turn pink. Roughly chop them.

Return the soup to the pan and reheat, then taste and season with salt, black pepper, cayenne pepper and lemon juice. Stir in the cream and reheat gently, adding the chopped prawns if using. Serve immediately, with a swirl of cream if you like.

Tips

- To get ahead, make the bisque in advance but don't add the prawns or cream. Cover and keep in the fridge overnight. When you're nearly ready to serve, cook the prawns and reheat the bisque until piping hot but not boiling, stirring in the cream as above.
- To make a bouquet garni, use kitchen string to tie together 1 bay leaf, 2 thyme sprigs and several parsley stalks, leaving some loose string to help you remove the bouquet.

Mussel and Saffron Soup

Serves **4**
Prep **30 mins**
Cook **25 mins**

GF Gluten-free

Mussels, leeks, saffron and cream have been a dream team for hundreds of years. *The Forme of Cury*, a collection of English recipes from the 14th century, includes a recipe for mussel, leek and saffron broth (thickened with ground almonds), which was adapted for the modern kitchen by Sara Paston-Williams in her book *The Art of Dining* (1993). Mussels are sustainable and fairly inexpensive, so you can splash out on the saffron for this luxurious soup.

1kg (2lb 3oz) live mussels in their shells

200ml (7fl oz) dry white wine

500ml (18fl oz) fish stock

40g (1½oz) butter

2 echalion shallots finely chopped

500g (1lb 2oz) leeks, trimmed (see Tip) and cut into 1–2cm (¾in) slices

1 garlic clove, chopped

Good pinch of saffron mixed with 2 tbsp just-boiled water

100ml (3½fl oz) double cream

Salt and pepper

Tip

Chop off the darker green parts of the leeks and use for stock. You need about 300g (10½oz) leeks for this soup.

Wash the mussels in cold water, scraping the shells to remove any barnacles and seaweed, and pulling out the beards. Discard any shells that are cracked, broken, or open and do not close when firmly tapped.

Put the wine in a large saucepan over a high heat and bring to the boil. Add the mussels, cover the pan and leave them to steam for 3–4 minutes, shaking or stirring once or twice until the shells have opened. Carefully tip the mussels and their cooking liquid into a colander over a bowl. Remove the mussels from their shells and set aside, discarding any that remain firmly closed. If you like, you can leave a few mussels in their shells to garnish.

Pour the mussel cooking liquid through a sieve lined with kitchen paper into a large measuring jug. Add the fish stock to make up the liquid to about 850ml (1½ pints).

Rinse out the saucepan and put over a medium-low heat. Add the butter and, when it begins to foam, add the shallots and a pinch of salt, and cook for 3–4 minutes, until softened.

Stir in the leeks, garlic and saffron water, cover and cook for a further 5 minutes until the leeks begin to soften. Pour in the fish and mussel stock and bring to the boil, then reduce the heat and simmer for 5–7 minutes until the leeks are just tender.

Remove 6 tablespoons of leeks and set aside. Blitz the contents of the pan with a stick blender thoroughly until smooth. Add the cream and blend again. Taste and adjust the seasoning, if necessary (you won't need much salt, if any).

Reheat gently, stir in the mussels and reserved leeks, and heat through without letting it boil. Serve immediately, garnished with the reserved mussels in their shells, if you like.

Clam Chowder

Serves **4**
Prep **30 mins, plus cleaning**
Cook **35–40 mins**

Although their shells are different, cockles and clams are interchangeable in many recipes, including this chowder. Chowders were first made in America by French fishermen who crossed the Atlantic to take advantage of the rich cod-fishing grounds south of Newfoundland. Into their large cooking pot (the *chaudière*, which gives the soup-stew its name), they added the ship's supplies of salt pork, 'ship's biscuit' (a very hard flour-and-water cracker made to survive long sea voyages) and onions, along with either the cod they had caught or the clams that were plentiful on the New England shores. In *Moby Dick* (1851), Ishmael and Queequeg enjoy a steaming chowder 'made of small juicy clams, scarcely bigger than hazel nuts, mixed with pounded ship biscuits, and salted pork cut up into little flakes; the whole enriched with butter, and plentifully seasoned with pepper and salt' – followed by a bowl of cod chowder. The chowder recipe diversified throughout the 19th century to include potatoes, milk, cream and, in some versions, tomatoes, corn and other vegetables.

1kg (2lb 3oz) live clams or cockles in their shells

40g (1½oz) butter

150g (5½oz) unsmoked bacon lardons or thick-cut streaky bacon, chopped

1 large onion, finely chopped

2 celery sticks, finely chopped

2 tbsp plain flour

300ml (10fl oz) milk, plus extra if needed

200g (7oz) potatoes, cut into 1cm (½in) dice

1 bay leaf

4–6 tbsp double cream, to taste

Pinch of cayenne pepper

1 tbsp chopped fresh parsley

Salt

Put the clams in a bowl of cold water, add a large pinch of salt and leave for 4 hours, or overnight, changing the water at least four times until it is clear.

Discard any clams that are broken, or open and do not close when firmly tapped. Pour 300ml (10fl oz) boiling water (from the kettle) into a large saucepan over a high heat and bring back to the boil. Add the clams, cover the pan and leave for 1 minute, then shake or stir and cook for a further 2 minutes or until the shells have opened.

Tip the clams and their cooking liquid into a colander over a large bowl. Pour the cooking liquid into a measuring jug through a sieve lined with kitchen paper to strain out any sand.

Melt half the butter in a saucepan over a medium-high heat, add the bacon and cook until golden and crisp. Using a slotted spoon, lift out the bacon and put on a plate.

Reduce the heat slightly, add the remaining butter, the onion and celery, and cook for 7–8 minutes until the vegetables have

softened. Stir in the flour and cook, stirring, for 2 minutes. Gradually stir in the clam cooking liquid and the milk, then add the potatoes and bay leaf. Bring to the boil, then reduce the heat, cover and simmer for 15 minutes or until the potatoes are tender. If the liquid is getting thick and gloopy, stir in a little more milk or boiling water.

While the potatoes are cooking, remove the clams from their shells, discarding any that remain firmly closed – beware, these may be full of sand.

Discard the bay leaf from the chowder and check the consistency: it should be rich and creamy but not too thick; adjust with a little more milk or boiling water if needed. Add the clams, cream, half the bacon and a pinch of cayenne, and warm through for a few minutes. Taste and add salt if necessary. Serve immediately, sprinkled with parsley and the remaining bacon.

Tip

Seashore foraging for shellfish can be fun and rewarding. Mussels attach themselves to rocks, while clams and cockles bury themselves just under the surface of sandy mudflats. You'll need to wash them well in several changes of water (it's advisable to do that even when they're shop-bought). Do your homework before foraging – ideally check several sources, locally and online – to be sure the beach is safe and unpolluted and that gathering shellfish for personal use is permitted.

Gumbo

Gumbo is famously a soup-stew in which anything goes – anything that could be found in and around Louisiana's waterways (bayous) and the Gulf Coast – from chicken, game birds and squirrel, to crayfish (crawdads), catfish, crabs and prawns (shrimp), with cured ham or sausage for extra flavour. Okra thickens the soup, so if you see small, bright-green fresh okra in a shop or market, think about putting it to use in a gumbo. This makes a substantial meal-in-a-bowl for four.

5 tbsp vegetable oil

1 large onion, finely chopped

2 celery sticks, finely diced

1 green pepper, deseeded and finely chopped

2 garlic cloves, finely chopped

200g (7oz) smoked sausage, sliced

1½ tsp smoked paprika

¼–½ tsp cayenne pepper, to taste

1½ tsp dried thyme

1½ tsp dried oregano

1 tsp salt

40g (1½oz) plain flour

500ml (18fl oz) hot chicken stock

2 bay leaves

400g (14oz) tin chopped tomatoes

140–175g (about 6oz) okra, topped and tailed, and cut into 1cm (½in) slices

200g (7oz) raw large prawns, peeled

Tabasco sauce, to taste

3 spring onions, finely sliced

2 tbsp chopped fresh parsley

Boiled rice and/or Cornbread Muffins (page 168), to serve

Heat 1 tablespoon of the oil in a large, heavy-based saucepan, then add the onion, celery and green pepper, and cook for 8–10 minutes until softened.

Add the garlic, sausage, spices, herbs and salt, and cook for 3 minutes, stirring to combine. Transfer the vegetable mixture to a plate.

Add the remaining oil to the pan, then gradually stir in the flour and cook over a low heat, stirring constantly, for 15 minutes or until the roux takes on a caramel colour.

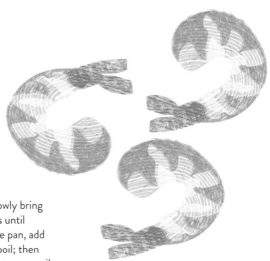

Gradually add the stock and bay leaves, and slowly bring to the boil, stirring constantly for 3–4 minutes until thickened. Return the vegetable mixture to the pan, add the tomatoes and okra, and bring back to the boil; then reduce the heat, cover and simmer for 15 minutes or until the okra is tender.

Add the prawns, cover the pan and cook for a few minutes, just until they turn opaque. Remove from the heat. Taste and add a dash or two of Tabasco for extra spicy heat.

If serving with rice, spoon the cooked rice into a small ramekin and then turn it out in the middle of each soup plate. Ladle the hot gumbo around the rice. Scatter over the spring onions and parsley and serve immediately – with cornbread muffins, if you like.

Tips

- You can make the gumbo in advance (or freeze it) without the prawns: add them only when you have reheated the gumbo to a steady simmer.
- Authentic recipes might use lard or dripping instead of vegetable oil; modern recipes often use butter.
- To make gumbo with chicken thighs or fresh sausages (as well as smoked sausage), brown them first, then remove and set aside while you cook the vegetables in the same pan. Continue as above, omitting the prawns if you prefer.
- If you have some Cajun spice mix, you can use 1–2 tablespoons, to taste, instead of the smoked paprika, cayenne, thyme, oregano and salt.

Leek Soup with Pan-Fried Scallops

Serves **4**
Prep **20 mins**
Cook **40 mins**

GF Gluten-free

Succulent scallops in a velvety green soup are perfect for an autumn dinner.

70g (2½oz) butter

1 onion or 4 shallots, finely chopped

800g (1¾lb) leeks, white and green parts separated, washed and thinly sliced (see Tip)

1 potato, cut into small dice

850ml (1½ pints) vegetable stock

4 tbsp double cream

Juice of ½ lemon or 1 lime

12 small fresh scallops, or 6 large ones

Salt and pepper

Melt 40g (1½oz) of the butter in a saucepan over a medium-low heat, add the onion, the whites of the leeks and a pinch of salt, and cook for 10 minutes or until softened.

Stir in the potato, then add the stock and another pinch of salt. Bring to the boil, then reduce the heat and simmer for 10–15 minutes until the potato is almost tender.

Bring the stock back to the boil, add the green parts of the leeks and simmer for 5–10 minutes until the potatoes and leeks are soft. Stir in the cream.

Blitz the soup with a stick blender until very smooth, then taste and adjust the seasoning, adding a squeeze of lemon juice to lift the flavour. For a really silky soup, rub it through a fine sieve.

Pat the scallops dry – if large, cut them in half horizontally. Season with salt and pepper. Put a frying pan over a high heat, add the remaining butter and, when it foams, add the scallops. Cook for 1–2 minutes on each side, until golden brown and just cooked through. Add a generous squeeze of lemon juice.

Reheat the soup without letting it boil, ladle into soup plates and put three scallops in each plate. Serve immediately.

Tips

- If the tops of your leeks are very tough, they will not cook through and will bring a coarse taste to the soup, so cut off the tough parts and set aside to add to vegetable stock.
- The green parts of the leeks give the soup its lovely green colour, so don't cook the soup for too long after you've added them or it will turn a drab olive colour.
- Get ahead by simmering the potatoes in the stock – leave the potatoes slightly underdone, as they will continue to soften in the stock. Cover and chill until nearly ready to serve, then bring back to the boil and add the green leeks; cook the scallops as above.

Cullen Skink

Serves **4**
Prep **20 mins**
Cook **30 mins**

 GF Gluten-free

Named after the fishing town of Cullen in north-east Scotland, the authentic version of this simple, comforting soup is made with finnan haddie, the local cold-smoked haddock, but any good undyed smoked haddock or other cold-smoked white fish works well.

40g (1½oz) butter

1 large onion, finely chopped

800ml (28fl oz) full-fat milk

1 bay leaf

450g (1lb) floury potatoes, cut into 1cm (½in) dice

450g (1lb) undyed smoked haddock, skin on

Salt and pepper

Snipped fresh chives, to garnish

Melt the butter in a saucepan over a medium-low heat, add the onion and a pinch of salt, and cook for 8–10 minutes until softened but not browned. Add the milk and bay leaf, bring to the boil, then add the potatoes, salt and pepper. Reduce the heat and simmer for 10–15 minutes until tender.

Cut the haddock into three or four large pieces and add to the pan in a single layer. Slowly bring the milk to a gentle simmer and cook for 2 minutes, then remove the pan from the heat, cover and leave to stand for 3–4 minutes until the fish is cooked. Using a slotted spoon, lift out the fish; flake the flesh, discarding the skin and bones, and set aside. Discard the bay leaf.

Remove about half the potatoes and onions and set aside with the fish.

Blitz the soup with a stick blender until smooth.

Return the fish, potatoes and onions to the soup and reheat without letting it boil. Taste and adjust the seasoning. Serve hot, garnished with chives.

Chilled Soups

Time to step out of your comfort zone. If you've been brought up on hot soups, you might think of cold soup as a modern interloper, but it has a long history, and it's not confined to hot countries. In Ukraine and its neighbouring countries, for example, borscht (beetroot soup) is served chilled as well as hot. *Koldskål* ('cold bowl') is a popular Danish soup, made from buttermilk – indeed, tartly refreshing dairy foods, such as buttermilk, yogurt and soured cream, are used in savoury and sweet cold soups throughout Europe and Western Asia.

Cold soups based on bread, garlic, olive oil, salt and vinegar have been eaten in the countries around the Mediterranean since ancient times, long before they took the name of gazpacho – and tomatoes didn't appear in the pot until the 19th century. In the sweltering summer heat, workers in the fields of southern Spain welcomed the arrival of the pot of gazpacho, which was cooled by evaporation from the unglazed earthenware vessel. In the rolling hills of eastern Poitou in France I've been offered *le mijet*: a soup of bread soaked in sharp red wine with a touch of sugar or honey, which once refreshed and nourished the region's agricultural workers.

Many rungs up the social ladder, chilled jellied consommé, sparkling in the candlelight, was often served as a first course at 19th-century dinner parties. Below stairs, skilled cooks had spent many hours preparing a soup that would be consumed in a couple of minutes.

Vichyssoise – creamy chilled leek and potato soup – is one of the best-known cold soups, and other vegetable soups, such as asparagus, pea or tomato, can be equally good served hot or cold.

Fruit soups predate smoothies by hundreds of years. Certain fruits and vegetables have particularly thirst-quenching properties: cucumbers and melons make simple soups for hot weather. Spiced apple and plum soups, both hot and cold, have been enjoyed since medieval times. In modern soups, sharp apples such as Bramley are sometimes paired with sweet root vegetables such as beetroot or parsnips. With their palate-awakening tartness, Hungarian sour cherry soup (*meggyleves*), Nordic blueberry soup (*blåbärssoppa*) and northern European red berry soup (*rødgrød* or *rote grütze*) are served as a first course, breakfast or dessert.

Just as hot soup should be served really hot, cold soups must be well chilled. Bear in mind that flavours are numbed by the cold, so don't hold back when tasting and adjusting the sharpness or sweetness before chilling. Chill your soup bowls or serving glasses too. Cold soups are often served in smaller quantities than hot soups, so serving them in small glasses can make them go further.

An obvious choice for summer meals, cold soups must be prepared in advance, so there's no last-minute cooking; just add a simple garnish of fresh herbs or edible flowers, or a slick of olive oil, depending on the soup. For barbecues – and parties at any time of year – pour the chilled soup into a big jug and serve in small tumblers.

Vichyssoise

Serves	**4**
Prep	**15 mins, plus chilling**
Cook	**40 mins**

V Vegetarian

GF Gluten-free

The classic luxurious chilled soup was created in the early 20th century by Louis Diat, a French chef working at the Ritz-Carlton hotel in New York. Inspired by his mother's homely leek and potato soup, to which she would sometimes add milk, he added cream and chilled his soup to appeal to his sophisticated customers.

40g (1½oz) butter

1 large onion, finely chopped

3–4 leeks, white and very pale green parts only, about 500g (1lb 2oz) trimmed weight, finely sliced (see Tip)

400g (14oz) floury potatoes, such as Maris Piper or King Edward, diced

800ml (28fl oz) vegetable or chicken stock

200ml (7fl oz) milk

100ml (3½fl oz) double cream

Salt and ground black, or white, pepper

Snipped chives, to garnish

Put a large saucepan over a medium-high heat and add the butter. When it foams, add the onion, leeks and a pinch of salt, then turn down the heat to low and cover the vegetables with a butter wrapper or a piece of baking paper. Cook for 10–15 minutes until softened, stirring from time to time.

Add the potatoes and cook for a minute or two, stirring to coat them in the onion and leek mixture. Add the stock and another pinch of salt, bring to the boil, then reduce the heat, cover and simmer for 20–25 minutes until the leeks and potatoes are soft.

Leave to cool slightly, add the milk, then blitz the soup with a stick blender until smooth. Rub the soup through a sieve into a bowl, then stir in the cream. Taste and season with salt and pepper – use white pepper, if you like. Cool, then chill for 3 hours. Serve with a sprinkling of chives.

Tips

- Vichyssoise is a pale, creamy soup, so cut off the green parts of the leeks and set them aside to make vegetable stock.
- The original vichyssoise was made with chicken stock, but vegetable stock is fine in this flavoursome soup.
- If you have some chive flowers, add them along with the chives for a pretty garnish.
- For an everyday leek and potato soup, serve this hot (no need to sieve it), with or without cream.

White Almond and Garlic Soup

Serves **4**
Prep **15 mins, plus chilling**

 Vegan

Much loved in Andalusia, where it is called *ajo blanco* ('white garlic'), this rich chilled soup is a refinement of the ancient, simple bread, garlic and olive oil soups of southern Europe. Almonds were introduced from the Middle East and planted in Italy, Provence and Spain. Imported to Britain from the 13th century, almonds were widely used in wealthy medieval households, with almond milk replacing animal milk on the many religious fast days throughout the year.

150g (5½oz) white bread, such as sourdough, crusts trimmed off

600ml (1 pint) ice-cold water

170g (6oz) blanched almonds (see Tip)

2 garlic cloves, roughly chopped

6 tbsp extra virgin olive oil, plus extra to serve

1½–2 tbsp sherry vinegar, to taste

Salt

12 green grapes (preferably Muscat), peeled and halved, seeds removed if necessary, to garnish

Put the bread in a bowl, cover it with the water and leave to soak for 5 minutes.

Put the almonds into a blender. Squeeze the bread so that some of the water drops back into the bowl, then add the moist bread to the almonds. Blitz, gradually adding the remaining water, the garlic, olive oil and 1 tablespoon of the sherry vinegar, blitzing until smooth. Season generously with salt to taste, adding a little more vinegar if you like. Transfer to a jug or bowl, cover and chill for at least 2 hours.

To serve, stir, then taste and adjust the seasoning, adding more salt or sherry vinegar if you like. Ladle the soup into bowls, add a drizzle of extra virgin olive oil and top with the halved grapes.

Tips

- If your almonds are still in their skins, it's easy to blanch them. Start with 185g (6¼oz), put them in a small bowl, pour boiling water over them and leave for 60 seconds (no more or they'll soften), then drain and rinse in cold water. Tip them onto a clean tea towel and rub off the skins: they will slip off easily.
- A garnish of fresh fruit is an important part of this summery dish. Muscat grapes are particularly aromatic, and peeling the grapes means that there is no tannic astringency.
- Diced melon, cucumber or apple would be alternative cool green toppings.
- It's a rich soup, intended to be served in small helpings.
- This is a good way to use up stale bread, although it's best to avoid the everyday 'white sliced' due to its rather gummy texture.

Courgette and Goat's Cheese Soup

Serves **4**
Prep **10 mins, plus chilling**
Cook **25 mins**

V Vegetarian
GF Gluten-free

When you have plenty of home-grown courgettes, or they're plentiful and local in the shops in the summer, this is a lovely simple soup to make. It's a great make-ahead first course for a dinner party and can be served in small cups or glasses.

200g (7oz) potatoes, cut into small dice
500ml (18fl oz) vegetable stock
500g (1lb 2oz) courgettes, diced
100g (3½oz) fresh goat's cheese, roughly chopped
Good pinch of paprika
Salt

Put the potatoes in a saucepan, pour in the stock and bring to the boil, then reduce the heat, cover and simmer for 10–15 minutes until almost tender.

Add the courgettes and simmer for a further 5–10 minutes until tender. Leave to cool slightly.

Add the goat's cheese and paprika, then blitz the soup with a stick blender until smooth. Taste and add a little more paprika and possibly some salt, depending on the saltiness of the stock and the goat's cheese. Cool, then chill for 3–4 hours. Serve with a sprinkling of paprika.

Tip

You could also serve this hot, with some extra goat's cheese scattered on top.

Serves **4–6**
Prep **30 mins, plus chilling**

 Vegan

Classic Gazpacho

There are probably as many ways of making this refreshing Spanish soup as there are cooks in Andalusia. This version was developed by the National Trust chefs. It's sometimes described as 'liquid salad' – the sweetness of the tomatoes is balanced with freshness from the cucumber and peppers, acidity from the vinegar and a kick of chilli.

80g (2¾oz) bread, torn into pieces

600g (1lb 5oz) ripe tomatoes, roughly chopped

½ cucumber, peeled and chopped

1 small green pepper, deseeded and chopped

1 small red pepper, deseeded and chopped

3 spring onions, roughly chopped

2 garlic cloves, roughly chopped

1 green chilli, deseeded and roughly chopped

A dash or two of Tabasco sauce (optional)

3 tbsp extra virgin olive oil, plus extra to serve

2 tbsp sherry vinegar, plus extra if needed

A good squeeze of lemon juice (optional)

1–2 tsp caster sugar, to taste (optional)

Sea salt and freshly ground black pepper

To serve

Ice cubes

Small Croutons (page 156)

1 small yellow pepper, deseeded and finely diced

1 small red pepper, deseeded and finely diced

½ cucumber, peeled, deseeded and finely diced

10 pitted black olives, quartered

Put the bread into a large bowl, add 100ml (3½fl oz) cold water and leave to soak for 30 minutes.

Meanwhile, prepare the vegetables. Put the tomatoes, cucumber, peppers, spring onions, garlic and chilli in a large bowl and mix everything together well.

Add the soaked bread, Tabasco, if using, olive oil, vinegar, salt and pepper, then mix again. Cover and put in the fridge to marinate for at least 30 minutes or overnight.

Blitz the soup with a stick blender until smooth, then chill for 3–4 hours (if it's already well chilled, it will only need another hour or so).

Taste the soup and add more Tabasco, vinegar, salt and pepper, and a little lemon juice or sugar, if needed, to balance the flavours. Serve the gazpacho in bowls, adding 3 ice cubes and a drizzle of olive oil to each bowl. Serve the croutons, diced peppers, cucumber and olives in small bowls for people to add their own garnish.

Tip

If your tomatoes are not 100 per cent ripe and full of flavour, you might like to add 1 tablespoon of tomato purée before you blitz the soup.

Watermelon Gazpacho

Serves **4–6**
Prep **15 mins, plus chilling**

 Vegetarian

 Gluten-free

Deep pink watermelon is wonderfully cooling on a hot day, especially in combination with cucumber and mint. Take this soup on a picnic in a wide-necked flask, or serve it for lunch or as a first course, topped with feta cheese, if you like.

200g (7oz) ripe red tomatoes

700g (1lb 9oz) peeled and seeded watermelon, cut into chunks (see Tip)

1 small red pepper, deseeded and chopped

½ small red onion, chopped

½ cucumber, peeled and chopped

15g (½oz) fresh mint leaves, plus extra to serve

2 tbsp extra virgin olive oil, plus extra to serve

2 tbsp sherry vinegar, plus extra if needed

1–2 tsp caster sugar, to taste (optional)

Sea salt and freshly ground black pepper

50–80g (2¾oz) feta cheese, crumbled, to serve (optional)

Cut the cores out of the tomatoes, then roughly chop the tomatoes and place in a blender.

Add the watermelon, red pepper, onion and cucumber to the blender, along with the mint, olive oil, sherry vinegar, a good pinch of salt and a grinding of black pepper. Blitz the soup thoroughly until smooth, then chill for 3–4 hours.

Taste the soup and add more vinegar, salt or a little sugar if needed to balance the flavours. Serve the gazpacho in bowls, topped with some crumbled feta, a little olive oil and a few small mint leaves.

Tip

Watermelons can vary enormously in size: some are so big that they are sold by the slice. For this recipe you need to weigh the watermelon after it's been peeled and the seeds removed. If you have some left over, wrap, chill and eat for breakfast or in a fruit salad the next day.

Strawberry Gazpacho

Serves **4–6**
Prep **15 mins, plus chilling**

 GF Gluten-free

Using fragrant summer strawberries and lime juice instead of sherry vinegar, this modern take on gazpacho is an elegant first course. Serve topped with fresh white crab meat or a spoonful of mascarpone cheese and lime zest – or you can keep it vegan with a little diced cucumber. Add cucumber-scented borage flowers if you have them: you can find them throughout the summer, from May to September.

200g (7oz) ripe red tomatoes

500g (1lb 2oz) ripe strawberries, hulled

1 small red pepper, deseeded and chopped

2 spring onions, chopped

1 small garlic clove, chopped

½ cucumber, peeled and chopped

8 basil leaves

2 tbsp extra virgin olive oil

Grated zest and juice of 1–2 limes, to taste

1–2 tsp caster sugar, to taste (optional)

Sea salt and freshly ground black pepper

To serve (your choice)

Small handful of borage flowers

4–6 tbsp mascarpone

100g (3½oz) white crab meat

Cut the cores out of the tomatoes, then roughly chop the tomatoes and place in a blender.

Add the strawberries, red pepper, spring onions, garlic and most of the cucumber to the blender, then add the basil, olive oil, the juice of 1 lime, a pinch of salt and a grinding of black pepper. Blitz the soup thoroughly until smooth, then chill for 3–4 hours.

Finely dice the reserved cucumber. Taste the soup and add more lime juice, salt and pepper, or a little sugar if needed to balance the flavours. Serve the gazpacho in bowls, adding some diced cucumber and a few borage flowers, if you like. Alternatively, add a spoonful of mascarpone or crab meat, and finish with a sprinkling of lime zest.

Tip

Try this if you have some frozen strawberries that need using up.

Creamy Cucumber Yogurt Soup

Serves **4**

Prep **15 mins, plus draining and chilling**

 V Vegetarian

GF Gluten-free

Cool as a cucumber, with the creamy tang of yogurt and the freshness of herbs, this simple soup is enjoyed in different versions all around the eastern Mediterranean. Pomegranate seeds are optional, adding colour, crunch and juicy tartness.

1 cucumber

600g (1lb 5oz) full-fat Greek-style yogurt

2 garlic cloves, grated

2 tbsp chopped fresh mint, plus a few small leaves to serve

2 tbsp chopped fresh dill, plus a few small fronds to serve

1–2 tbsp fresh lemon juice, to taste

A little chilled vegetable stock, if needed

Salt and pepper

To serve

Extra virgin olive oil or cold-pressed rapeseed oil

½ pomegranate (optional), seeds removed

Using a vegetable peeler, peel off alternate strips of the cucumber skin (see Tip). Cut in half lengthways and use a teaspoon to scrape out most of the seeds. Grate into a colander, sprinkle with salt and leave for 30 minutes. Rinse briefly under cold water and gently press out the excess water with a clean tea towel.

Put the cucumber in a large bowl. Add the yogurt, garlic, herbs and 1 tablespoon of the lemon juice. Stir, then season with salt and pepper to taste. Cover the bowl and chill for at least 30 minutes.

To serve, stir, then taste and adjust the seasoning, adding more lemon juice if you like. You may want to adjust the consistency by adding a little chilled water or vegetable stock. Garnish with a drizzle of oil, a few small dill fronds and mint leaves, and pomegranate seeds, if you like.

Tips

- Add the leftover peeled strips of cucumber skin to a jug of chilled water to make it extra refreshing.
- Mint always goes well with cucumber. If dill is not available, or you don't like it, try flat-leaf parsley, chives, tarragon or coriander.
- You can use dried mint instead of fresh: use 1 tablespoon dried mint and leave out the dill.
- If you have a large cucumber, you could set aside a 7cm (2¾in) piece and cut it into tiny dice to garnish the soup.
- Supermarkets often sell ready-prepared pomegranate seeds. They are a great time saver, but not cheap. If you want to remove the seeds from a pomegranate, cut it in half, then hold over a bowl and tap firmly with a rolling pin to collect the seeds. Pick through and remove the white pith, which can taste bitter.

Green Salad Soup

Serves   **2**
Prep   **10 mins,
          plus chilling**

 Vegan

Do you have overripe avocado, forgotten salad or leftover herbs? Give them a Cinderella makeover for this herb-packed, summery soup; but remember: no amount of magic will help the ugly sisters, so discard any black and stringy bits of avocado, and give your salad a quick sort through, jettisoning any leaves that you really wouldn't want to put in your mouth. Cherry tomatoes add a juicy burst of colour, and garlic breadcrumbs or mixed seeds and nuts bring contrasting crunch.

1 ripe avocado

Grated zest and juice of 1 lime or lemon

200g (7oz) mixed salad leaves, preferably including some watercress, baby spinach or rocket

Large handful of soft herbs, such as parsley or coriander (see Tip)

1 garlic clove, roughly chopped

4 spring onions, roughly chopped

A handful of frozen peas

Salt and pepper

To serve

Cherry tomatoes, halved

Extra virgin olive oil

Garlic Breadcrumbs (page 157) or Toasted Seeds (page 158)

Halve the avocado and scoop the flesh into a food processor or blender. Add half the lime zest and juice, then add the leaves, herbs, garlic, spring onions, peas, a little salt and pepper and 150ml (5fl oz) cold water. Blitz the soup until smooth.

Taste and add more lime juice, salt or pepper if needed. You may like to add a splash more cold water to adjust the consistency. Chill for 1–2 hours.

Serve in soup plates or bowls, topped with cherry tomatoes, a drizzle of olive oil and a sprinkling of garlic breadcrumbs.

Tips

• If your mixed salad includes radicchio or other red leaves, pick out the larger ones before blending the soup so that it keeps a vibrant green colour.

• Parsley or coriander are good basic herbs for this soup, and mint (anything from a few leaves to a small handful) adds freshness. Or try chervil, basil or oregano – it's best to stick to two or, at most, three different herbs.

• Look for packs of 'salad sprinkles': mixed seeds and nuts that boost the nutritional content of soups, salads and bakes.

Chilled Tomato and Basil Soup with Burrata and Basil Oil

Serves **4**

Prep **10 mins, plus chilling**

Cook **15 mins**

 Vegetarian

 Gluten-free

With its intense flavours, this twist on a tomato, basil and mozzarella salad is perfect for a summer lunch or dinner.

1 tbsp olive oil

3 echalion shallots, finely chopped

1 garlic clove, chopped

900g (2lb) ripe tomatoes, roughly chopped

500ml (18fl oz) vegetable stock

Good handful of basil

Lemon juice, red wine vinegar or balsamic vinegar (optional)

1–2 tsp caster sugar, to taste (optional)

Salt and freshly ground black pepper

To serve

1 burrata or 2 buffalo mozzarella cheeses

Basil Oil (page 152)

Balsamic vinegar

Heat the olive oil in a large saucepan, add the shallots, a pinch of salt and some freshly ground black pepper, and cook for 4–5 minutes until softened. Add the garlic, tomatoes and stock, bring almost to the boil, then reduce the heat to low and simmer for 5 minutes. Leave to cool slightly.

Meanwhile, finely chop the basil stalks and tear the leaves. Reserve a few small basil leaves to garnish.

Add the basil to the soup and leave to infuse for 10–15 minutes. Blitz the soup using a stick blender, then rub through a fine sieve over a bowl to remove the tomato skins and seeds. Taste the soup and add more salt and pepper, plus lemon juice, vinegar or sugar if needed to balance the flavours. Cool, then chill for 3–4 hours.

Taste the chilled soup and adjust the seasoning.

Cut the burrata into four, or tear the buffalo mozzarella into spoon-sized pieces. Spoon the tomato soup into four soup plates. Top with the cheese, then drizzle over the basil oil and balsamic vinegar, grind over some black pepper and scatter over the reserved basil leaves.

Tips

- Reheat gently to serve as a simple hot tomato and basil soup.
- Briefly cooking the tomatoes with their skins on gives an intense flavour – it's worth the little extra time it takes to pass the soup through a sieve to remove the skins at the end.

Peach and Lavender Soup

Serves **4**
Prep **15 mins, plus cooling and chilling**
Cook **30 mins, and 1 hour for the meringues**

 V Vegetarian

 GF Gluten-free

A pretty, do-ahead dessert with a subtle waft of lavender. Use peaches or nectarines; if they're not quite ripe, you can ripen them in the fruit bowl for a day or two until they're fragrant, but don't let them over-ripen. Mini meringues add a crisp texture, but if it sounds like too much faff to make them, you could use bought mini-meringues or simply decorate the soup with a splash of strawberry sauce or a few thinly sliced ripe strawberries.

115g (4oz) sugar

2 tbsp honey

3 lavender sprigs (see Tip) or 2 tsp dried lavender flowers

2 lemons: strips of peel pared off 1 lemon, juice squeezed from both

6 peaches or nectarines, about 750g (1lb 10oz), halved, stones removed

Mini meringues

2 egg whites, at room temperature

100g (3½oz) caster sugar

¼ tsp white wine vinegar

Strawberry sauce

150g (5½oz) strawberries, hulled, roughly chopped

4 tsp icing sugar, plus extra if needed

1 tsp lemon juice, plus extra if needed

Put the sugar, honey, lavender and two strips of lemon peel in a wide saucepan that will hold the peaches in a single layer. Add 1 litre (1¾ pints) water and half the lemon juice, then bring to the boil, stirring to dissolve the sugar. Reduce the heat, cover and simmer for 10 minutes.

Add the peaches, cover and simmer for 10–20 minutes, until they are soft when tested with the tip of a sharp knife.

Using a slotted spoon, remove the peaches from the liquid and put on a tray to cool, spacing them apart.

Remove the lemon peel from the poaching liquid and boil the liquid until it has reduced to about 600ml (1 pint). Strain through a fine sieve into a measuring jug – the syrup will be a lovely rosy colour.

When the fruit is cool enough to handle, gently peel off the skins. Roughly chop the fruit and put in a blender.

Pour about three-quarters of the syrup into the blender. Blitz until smooth, then taste and add a little more syrup or lemon juice to make a sweet yet fresh-tasting soup. Transfer to a covered container. Cool, then chill for at least 2 hours.

To make the meringues, preheat the oven to 120°C/110°C fan/ gas ½ and line a large baking sheet with baking paper.

Using an electric whisk, beat the egg whites in a clean bowl until soft peaks form. Whisk in the sugar 1 tablespoon at a time, whisking well between each addition. Add the vinegar with the last of the sugar and beat until thick and glossy. Spoon the meringue mix into a piping bag fitted with a star nozzle and pipe small meringues, 3cm (1¼in) in diameter, onto the prepared baking sheet. Bake for 10 minutes. Turn the oven down to 100°C/90°C fan/gas ¼ and bake for a further 45–50 minutes, until set and crisp: it will be easy to lift a meringue off the paper. Turn the oven off and leave the meringues to cool in the oven.

To make the strawberry sauce, put the ingredients into a food processor or blender and blitz to a purée. (Alternatively, rub them through a sieve into a bowl.) Taste and add more sugar and lemon juice to get a sweet-sharp sauce.

Taste the chilled soup: you may want to add a little more syrup or lemon juice. Serve in soup plates, topped with a few meringues and a drizzle of strawberry sauce.

Tips

- If using fresh lavender, rinse it in a little salted water to draw out any bugs, then pat dry.
- Store leftover egg yolks in a sealed container in the fridge for up to 3 days.
- To freeze egg yolks, beat with a small pinch of salt or a generous pinch of caster sugar, date and label 'salt' or 'sweet' and freeze for up to 2 months.

Melon and Mint Soup

Serves **4–6**
Prep **10 mins, plus chilling**

V0 Vegan
GF Gluten-free

Perfumed, sweet, juicy cantaloupe melons are a real treat in the summer months. As a first course they're served in wedges, often with cured ham; as a dessert they're delicious teamed with strawberries in fruit salad. This soup makes a wonderfully refreshing starter or dessert: choose your seasonings and garnishes accordingly.

2 ripe cantaloupe melons, such as Charentais

5–6 mint sprigs, to taste

Juice of 2–3 limes or lemons, to taste

Sea salt (optional)

Freshly ground black pepper

Halve the melons, then scoop out and discard the seeds. Scoop out the flesh, roughly chop and put it in a food processor or blender.

Remove the leaves from the mint sprigs, setting aside a few leaves to garnish.

Add the mint leaves to the blender, along with about half the lime or lemon juice. Blend in short bursts until smooth, then taste and add more lime juice and a pinch of salt if needed. Chill for 3–4 hours.

To garnish, pile the reserved mint leaves on top of each other, roll up lengthways and then cut into thin strips

Serve the soup in bowls or small glasses, adding a few shredded mint leaves, plus a grinding of black pepper for a first course.

Tips

- It's important to use ripe melons, but if you buy them a few days before you need them, they will continue to ripen at room temperature in your kitchen. To check for ripeness, gently press the base (the opposite end to the stem): it should have a bit of give and will smell fragrant.
- You could use basil instead of mint if making this as a first course; start with 15–20 leaves, adding more to taste.
- If the soup doesn't have to be vegan, sprinkle some chopped prosciutto (or Prosciutto Crisps, see page 164) on top.

Red Fruit Soup

Serves **4**
Prep **15 mins, plus chilling**
Cook **15 mins**

V Vegetarian
GF Gluten-free

Much loved in Denmark, as *rødgrød*, this fruit soup is also known in Germany as *rote grütze*, which means 'red groats': a reminder that it was once made with oatmeal. Cornflour replaces the oats as a thickener in this simple dessert soup of fresh summer berries. It is usually served with a generous swirl of cream. It's like summer pudding, but without the bread!

250g (9oz) cherries, stoned

250g (9oz) redcurrants

250g (9oz) raspberries

85g (3oz) caster sugar, plus extra to sprinkle

4 tbsp cornflour

Juice of ½ lemon (optional)

To serve

Double cream

A few borage flowers (optional)

Put all the fruit in a saucepan. Add the sugar and 250ml (9fl oz) water and put over a medium heat, then bring to a simmer for about 7 minutes.

Mix the cornflour with 4 tablespoons of water until smooth. Stir the cornflour mixture into the fruit, then simmer for 2–3 minutes, stirring until the mixture has thickened. Pour it into a bowl. Add 100ml (3½fl oz) just-boiled water to the pan, stirring to loosen the remaining fruit mixture, then tip it into the bowl and stir well. Sprinkle a little sugar over the top to prevent a skin from forming and leave to cool, then chill for at least 2 hours.

Taste the chilled fruit soup. You might want to add a squeeze of lemon juice to lift and balance the flavours. Serve in soup plates with plenty of cream poured over. Decorate with borage flowers, if you like.

Tips

- The fruits listed above are just a suggestion: if you have only a small amount of redcurrants, add more of another fruit, such as strawberries (quartered if large), loganberries, blackcurrants or blackberries. Some recipes include gooseberries. If you're a successful forager (see page 48) you could include bilberries or elderberries – but only pick elderberries if they're ripe, otherwise they will be very sour.

- In winter, this can be made with frozen mixed berries (cook from frozen for about 15 minutes) and a good pinch of ground cinnamon; serve warm.

- If you like, stir 1–2 tablespoons of cherry brandy, to taste, into the chilled soup.

- If you have any leftover soup, serve for breakfast with yogurt.

Stocks, Garnishes and Accompaniments

Most soups originate in the stockpot, gently simmering over the heat for hours and yielding a liquid full of flavour and nutrients. Many cooks insist that you can't make good soup without good stock. There are many interpretations of what makes a good stock, but all agree that while it shouldn't be complicated, it can't be rushed either. That said, you can make a perfect vegetable stock or fish stock from scratch in less than an hour, and vegetable stock forms the base of many a thrifty soup. Bouillon powder and stock cubes are quick and convenient, but they can make your soups taste samey and are often salty. You can dodge this by diluting them far more than recommended on the packet: try using half a stock cube next time you need stock; taste it before adding it to your soup; you might want to dilute it even more to avoid saltiness.

Welcome and warming (or cooling) as a soup may be, a garnish makes it even more appealing. Consider ways to introduce another colour or texture; add cool yogurt to a spicy soup to bring a contrasting temperature, or pesto to introduce another flavour dimension. A swirl of cream or herb oil, a spoonful of whipped cream or crème fraîche sprinkled with herbs, a few crunchy seeds or chopped nuts, a flash of freshness from a tangy salsa, or a splash of colour from a nasturtium flower all enhance the taste as well as adding colour. Or you can style up your soups with a combination of two or three garnishes. One thing to remember, however, is that no matter how satisfyingly crunchy your croutons or other crispy additions might be, they'll soften as soon as they meet the soup. The way round this is to serve them in a small bowl for people to add, a few at a time, at the table.

Soups can easily be a meal in themselves – they're a very popular choice in the National Trust cafés, where they're served with a hunk of crusty bread or a cheese scone. In this chapter you'll find recipes for scones, soda bread, gluten-free cornbread and buttery cheese biscuits.

Light Chicken Stock

Makes	about 1.2 litres (2 pints)
Prep	15 mins, plus cooling
Cook	1 hour

Don't waste the carcass of a roasted chicken (or duck, or pheasant). Use it to make this stock – there will be enough to make a good soup.

1 roast chicken carcass, broken into pieces

1 onion, roughly chopped

1 large carrot, roughly chopped

1 celery stick, roughly chopped

1 bay leaf

10 black peppercorns

A few fresh parsley stalks or thyme sprigs (optional)

Pinch of salt

Put the chicken bones into a large saucepan or stockpot and add cold water to cover, about 1.5 litres (2½ pints). Add the remaining ingredients, cover with a lid and bring to the boil over a medium-high heat, then reduce the heat so that the liquid simmers gently. Skim off the scum that rises to the top. Simmer for at least 1 hour (see Tips).

Leave to cool slightly. Place a colander or sieve over a bowl and ladle the liquid into the sieve (using a ladle prevents splashing). When you have ladled out most of the liquid, tip the bones and vegetables into the sieve and leave to drain and cool. Leave in a cool place until the fat rises to the surface. Spoon off as much of the fat as you can, or place in the fridge overnight; the next day you'll be able to lift off the fat easily (keep the fat in the fridge and use it for frying onions or roasting potatoes).

Store in the fridge for a couple of days or in the freezer for up to 3 months.

Ham Stock

Use the bone from a baked or boiled ham (gammon joint) instead of chicken.

Tips

• Add a leek, or some green leek tops, mushroom stalks, thyme sprigs or fennel trimmings, if you have them.

• You can leave the stock simmering for 2–3 hours to extract even more goodness, flavour and body.

• If you're short of freezer space, simmer the strained and defatted stock to reduce it by half or more before freezing. Remember to add more water to dilute the stock when you come to use it.

• A pressure cooker saves time and fuel. Follow the manufacturer's instructions – you will need less liquid as it takes less time to extract the flavour from the chicken – and cook for 30 minutes at high pressure. Cool quickly, then strain as above.

Rich Chicken Stock

Makes **about 1.5 litres (2½ pints)**
Prep **15 mins, plus cooling**
Cook **3–3½ hours**

If you have more time, you can make this stock, which is fuller in flavour and body than the Light Chicken Stock. It uses chicken wings, which are reasonably cheap, or your butcher might give you some chicken bones for nothing. You can keep raw bones in the freezer until you have enough to make this stock. It needs longer simmering so it's worth making a decent amount.

1kg (2lb 3oz) chicken wings and bones

2 onions, roughly chopped

2 carrots, roughly chopped

100ml (3½fl oz) red wine or dry white wine (optional)

2 celery sticks, roughly chopped

2–3 garlic cloves, to taste, lightly crushed

2 bay leaves

10 black peppercorns

A few fresh parsley stalks or thyme sprigs (optional)

Pinch of salt

Tips

• If you have them, add green leek tops, mushroom stalks, thyme sprigs or fennel trimmings.

• After roasting, you can add all the ingredients to a pressure cooker and cook for 30–40 minutes at high pressure (check the manufacturer's instructions). Cool quickly, then strain as above.

Preheat the oven to 200°C/180°C fan/gas 6. Put the wings and bones, onions and carrots in a deep roasting tin and roast for 20–25 minutes, then turn everything over and roast for a further 20–25 minutes until golden brown.

Using a slotted spoon, put the contents of the roasting tin into a large saucepan or stockpot. Pour off the fat into a bowl and keep it in the fridge for cooking. Add the wine or some just-boiled water to the roasting tin and stir to dislodge the tasty browned bits, then add this liquid to the pan. Add cold water to cover, about 1.7 litres (3 pints), then add the remaining ingredients. Cover with a lid and bring to the boil over a medium-high heat, then reduce the heat so that the liquid simmers gently. Skim off the scum that rises to the top. Simmer very gently for 2–2½ hours.

Leave to cool slightly. Place a colander or sieve over a bowl and ladle the liquid into the sieve (using a ladle prevents splashing). When you have ladled out most of the liquid, tip the bones and vegetables into the sieve and leave to drain and cool.

When cool, spoon off as much of the fat as you can, or place the stock in the fridge overnight; the next day you'll be able to lift off the fat easily (keep the fat in the fridge and use it for frying onions or roasting potatoes).

Beef Stock

Make as above but start with about 1.5kg (3½lb) beef bones or oxtail (the narrow end with less meat is fine) instead of the chicken. If you ask in advance, your butcher should be able to save you some beef bones; ask them to crack the bones, which is easy for them to do with their cleaver and block.

Light Vegetable Stock

Quick and easy to make, this is a useful multipurpose stock. Chop the veg quite small to extract the maximum flavour.

Makes **about 1.3 litres (2¼ pints)**

Prep **10 mins, plus cooling**

Cook **40 mins**

 Vegan

GF Gluten-free

2 onions, chopped

2 leeks, sliced

2 carrots, chopped

2 celery sticks, chopped

1 bay leaf

10 black peppercorns

A few fresh parsley stalks or thyme sprigs (optional)

Put all the ingredients into a large saucepan or stockpot and add cold water to cover – about 1.5 litres (2½ pints). Bring to the boil, then reduce the heat, cover and simmer gently for 30–40 minutes.

Leave to cool for 10 minutes. Place a colander or sieve over a bowl and ladle the liquid into the sieve (using a ladle prevents splashing). When you have ladled out most of the liquid, tip the vegetables into the sieve and leave to drain and cool.

Store in the fridge for a couple of days or in the freezer for up to 3 months.

Tips

- Add other vegetable odds and ends, such as chopped fresh tomato or tomato skins, mushrooms or mushroom stalks, pea or broad bean pods, asparagus or fennel trimmings.
- Avoid using potatoes and strongly flavoured vegetables such as swede, parsnips, cabbage and broccoli.
- Foragers may like to add a few well-washed young nettle leaves or a piece of kelp; kelp is also known as *kombu* and is often used in Japanese stocks and soups.
- If you're not vegetarian or vegan, you could add Parmesan rind (or other hard cheese rinds) to your stock for a savoury flavour; fish it out before you strain the stock.

Rich Vegetable Stock

Makes **about 1.3 litres (2¼ pints)**

Prep **15 mins, plus cooling**

Cook **about 1 hour**

V0 Vegan

GF Gluten-free

If you have a little more time you can make this full-bodied stock, perfect for onion soup, minestrone and many other vegetable, lentil and bean soups.

1 tbsp olive oil

2 onions, roughly chopped

2 leeks, or green leek tops, sliced

2 carrots, chopped

2 celery sticks, chopped

4 tbsp dry white wine (optional)

2 garlic cloves, halved (optional)

1 bay leaf

10 black peppercorns

A few fresh parsley stalks or thyme sprigs (optional)

Heat the oil in a large saucepan, add the onions, leeks, carrots and celery, and cook for 15 minutes or until softened and golden.

Add the wine, if using, or a splash of cold water, and stir well, scraping up any browned bits into the liquid. Add the garlic, if using, bay leaf, peppercorns and herbs, then pour on cold water to cover, about 1.5 litres (2½ pints). Stir and bring to the boil. Skim off any foam, then reduce the heat, cover and simmer gently for 30–40 minutes.

Leave to cool slightly, then strain through a fine sieve.

Store in the fridge for a couple of days or in the freezer for up to 3 months.

Tips

- Add 100g (3½oz) mushrooms or mushroom trimmings when browning the veg.
- Deepen the flavour by adding a dab of Marmite or miso (dissolved in a splash of just-boiled water) or a dash of soy sauce to your strained stock.
- If you're not vegan, add a piece of Parmesan rind (or a vegetarian hard cheese rind) to your stock along with the bay leaf.
- You can concentrate the flavour by simmering the strained stock for a further 15 minutes or so. Add peas, diced carrots, sliced mushrooms, broccoli, shredded cabbage, ginger or garlic for a nourishing lunchtime broth.

Fish Stock

Whenever you buy fish, ask your fishmonger to give you some extra backbones and heads from white fish – but check that they are very fresh and don't smell at all 'fishy'.

Makes **about 1.3 litres (2¼ pints)**
Prep **15 mins**
Cook **30 mins**

 Gluten-free

800g (1¾lb) white fish bones and heads, roughly chopped
1 onion, finely chopped
1 celery stick, finely chopped
1 bay leaf
Handful of parsley stalks
6 peppercorns
Juice of ½ lemon

Rinse the fish bones and heads to remove any blood. Drain and place in a large saucepan or stockpot, along with the remaining ingredients.

Add just enough cold water to cover, about 1.5 litres (2½ pints), and bring slowly to the boil. Skim off any scum, then cover the pan, reduce the heat and simmer very gently for 30 minutes (see Tips).

Leave to cool for 15 minutes, then strain and leave to cool completely. Keep in the fridge for up to 2 days or freeze for up to 3 months.

Tips

- Don't use oily fish, such as salmon, red mullet or mackerel.
- If using fish heads, check that the gills have been removed.
- If you don't have enough fish bones, freeze the bones as you buy them until you get some more.
- Keep the stock barely simmering: don't let it boil, or it will become bitter.
- If you like, add some fennel trimmings or ½ teaspoon fennel seeds, a few sprigs of thyme or tarragon, a star anise, or 150ml (5fl oz) dry white wine.

Garnishes

Finely chopped parsley is a classic soup garnish for good reason: it adds a fresh taste and a bright green colour, it's rich in nutrients, it's easy to grow and it's readily available throughout the summer and into the autumn. Other fresh herbs bring their own subtle flavours and visual interest: oniony chives, warmly fragrant basil, aromatic coriander, mildly aniseed-like chervil and dill.

Fresh edible flowers can add the wow factor for free if you have any of the following in your garden: pansies, primroses, bright orange and yellow peppery-flavoured nasturtiums and pot marigold petals (*Calendula officinalis*), as well as the flowers of herbs such as borage, chives, marjoram and rosemary. Foraging (see page 48) may yield the starry white flowers of wild garlic, or the bright yellow petals of gorse or dandelion.

Thinly sliced spring onions add their savoury flavour to a wide range of soups; thinly sliced radishes or cauliflower florets provide contrasting colour and texture; tiny black and white sesame seeds look dramatic, as do nigella seeds – and the warmth of the soup brings out their gentle oniony flavour.

Another idea that uses the heat of the soup to add extra savoury flavour is to sprinkle over some crumbled goat's cheese or feta cheese, or nutritional yeast flakes.

Sometimes a soup calls out for crunch. The ideas for crispy bits (see pages 160–65) can be used on their own or in combination with other garnishes. If time is short, you can buy mixed vegetable crisps, tortilla chips and poppadoms to do the job, or try toasted nuts (see page 159). If you eat meat, diced bacon, pancetta and chorizo, fried until crisp and drained, are delicious scattered over soups and chowders.

Soups are generally low in fat, so a swirl of cream can add a touch of richness that enhances the flavour of many. A spoonful of whipped cream, soured cream or crème fraîche, or a plant-based alternative such as coconut cream, has a similar effect. And if your soup is on the spicy side, thick Greek-style yogurt is wonderfully cooling.

Extra virgin olive oil has a peppery flavour that enhances many soups, especially those made with Mediterranean vegetables such as tomatoes, fennel and peppers. Drizzle it over the soup just before serving.

Herb and Spice Oils

Drizzled over soup just before serving, herb and spice oils add colour and fragrance to enhance the dish.

Basil Oil

You can also use other soft herbs, such as parsley, mint or coriander, in this recipe.

You will need a handful of herbs. Fill a small bowl with ice-cold water. Discard the tougher stems from the herbs or, if using mint, pick the leaves off the woody stems. You will need a small fistful of the prepared herbs.

Bring a small saucepan of water to a rolling boil and blanch the herbs for 10 seconds, then immediately transfer them to the ice-cold water using a slotted spoon. Drain well in a colander and then on a clean tea towel, pressing out as much moisture as you possibly can. Chop the herbs roughly, then blitz them with 5 tablespoons vegetable oil (if you like, use olive oil when making basil oil) until you have a bright green oil. Stir in a tiny pinch of salt.

Store in a covered container in the fridge for up to 3 days.

Rosemary Oil

You can also use other woody herbs, such as sage and thyme, in this recipe.

Pick the leaves from a few sprigs of rosemary and gently pinch them to release some of their aroma. Heat 4 tablespoons extra virgin olive oil (or cold-pressed rapeseed oil) in a small saucepan over a medium heat. Add the herbs and heat until they just begin to sizzle. Take the pan off the heat and leave to cool, then strain.

Store in a lidded sterilised jar or bottle for up to 1 month.

Tip

You can also make spice oils this way: lightly crush coriander, cumin or fennel seeds before adding them to the warm oil. Finely chopped fresh red chilli or dried chilli flakes work well too; add a pinch of paprika, smoked if you like, to enhance the red colour.

Flavoured Butters

In France, butter is sometimes stirred into thick vegetable soups just before serving; it's the northern equivalent of the slick of olive oil added to soups in the south. Keep one or two of these butters in the fridge (for up to 3 days) or the freezer (for up to 1 month), ready to slice and serve on a hot soup.

Parsley and Garlic Butter

60g (2¼oz) unsalted butter, softened

2 tbsp chopped fresh parsley

2 garlic cloves, crushed

Salt and pepper

Blue Cheese Butter

60g (2¼oz) unsalted butter, softened

30g (1oz) blue cheese, such as Stilton or Gorgonzola, crumbled

1 tbsp chopped fresh parsley

Ground black pepper

Chilli Butter

60g (2¼oz) unsalted butter, softened

½–1 red chilli, to taste, deseeded and finely chopped, or a pinch of dried chilli flakes

2 tbsp finely chopped fresh coriander

Salt and pepper

Put all the ingredients in a small bowl and use a fork to mash them together. Place in the fridge to firm up, then scrape the butter onto a piece of baking paper and roll up into a cylindrical shape. Return to the fridge for at least 2 hours, until firm. To serve, cut into 8mm (⅜in) slices and add to the soup just before serving.

Gremolata

A mix of parsley, lemon zest and garlic, this topping adds freshness to soups made with squash and root veg, or you can try it with Spelt and Borlotti Bean Soup (page 72), or Scotch Broth (page 85) instead of using plain parsley.

Dry the parsley thoroughly before you chop it. If you have one, a mezzaluna makes quick work of finely chopping herbs.

Grated zest of 1 lemon

2 tbsp finely chopped flat-leaf parsley

½ small garlic clove, finely grated

Mix the ingredients together in a small bowl. Use on the day you make it.

Pesto

Serves **4**
Prep **10 mins**
Cook **3–4 mins**

GF Gluten-free

The sauce we think of as classic pesto (*pesto alla Genovese*), made from basil, pine nuts and Parmesan or pecorino cheese, has in the past been made from walnuts and garlic, or parsley, marjoram and Dutch cheese. The myriad versions found today – such as coriander and pistachio or carrot top and cashew – are just continuing the tradition of making use of what's available. The word 'pesto' simply means 'pounded' (as with a pestle).

40g (1½oz) pine nuts

Bunch of basil leaves, about 30g (1oz)

1 small garlic clove, halved

40g (1½oz) finely grated Parmesan

½ lemon, to taste

4–6 tbsp extra virgin olive oil, as needed

Salt

Toast the pine nuts in a dry, heavy-based pan over a medium heat for 3 minutes or until they are aromatic. Leave to cool.

Put the basil, pine nuts, garlic, cheese, a squeeze of lemon juice and a pinch of salt into a food processor or blender, and pulse briefly to combine.

Add 4 tablespoons of the oil and blend to a coarse paste, adding more if needed. Taste and add a squeeze more of lemon juice and a little more salt, if you like. Transfer to a jar.

To store, put in a sealed container and add a thin layer of olive oil over the pesto, then keep in the fridge for up to 3 days. Stir before using.

Tips

- For vegan pesto, replace the cheese with 3 tablespoons of nutritional yeast flakes and make sure that you add a good squeeze of lemon juice. Alternatively, from the increasing range of plant-based cheeses, choose a sharp-flavoured hard cheese that can be finely grated.
- You can use a vegetarian alternative to Parmesan.
- If using a pestle and mortar, grind the nuts first, then grind in the garlic and salt, then the basil, and then the oil. Finally, stir in the cheese.
- Instead of pine nuts, try (unsalted) almonds, cashew nuts, hazelnuts, walnuts or sunflower seeds. If using harder nuts, such as almonds and walnuts, roughly chop the toasted nuts before adding them to the blender.
- Instead of basil, try soft herbs such as parsley, coriander and rocket. You could also include chervil, mint, watercress or spinach in the mix.
- For 'no-waste' pesto, use well-washed fresh green carrot tops, kale or chopped broccoli stems. It's easier to make these in a blender rather than using a pestle and mortar.
- Experiment with other cheeses: for example, parsley, Cheddar and hazelnut make a delicious 'English pesto'.

Dumplings

Serves **4–6**
Prep **5 mins**
Cook **15 mins**

 V Vegetarian

Make your dumplings small (walnut sized) so that they cook quickly and become light rather than leaden. Matzo balls (page 100) are a delightful dumpling alternative. All work well in clear broths, or you can add them to a well-flavoured homemade stock for a simple lunchtime soup. Dumplings are also a great addition to Goulash Soup (page 108) and Beetroot and Horseradish Soup (page 31).

100g (3½oz) self-raising flour, plus extra for dusting

50g (1¾oz) shredded vegetable suet

1 tbsp finely chopped fresh parsley or chives, or 2 tsp finely chopped fresh thyme, sage or rosemary, or 1 tsp grated fresh horseradish (optional)

Salt and pepper

Mix all the ingredients together in a bowl, then add enough cold water, 4–5 tablespoons, to make a firm but pliable dough. Flour your hands, then divide the dough into 12–16 walnut-sized pieces and roll into small balls.

Place the dumplings on top of your simmering soup, cover the pan and simmer for 15 minutes or until light and fluffy. Serve immediately.

Tip

You can make the dumplings up to 24 hours ahead and keep them, spaced apart, on a lightly floured tray in the fridge.

Croutons

Serves   **4–6**
Prep   **5–10 mins**
Cook   **5–10 mins**

 Vegan

When bread loses its plump freshness and begins to dry out, make croutons. Sprinkle a few over your soup – not too many at a time or they'll go soggy – and serve the rest in a small bowl.

3 slices slightly stale white bread, such as sourdough, crusts removed

2 tbsp olive oil, rapeseed oil or flavoured oil, such as garlic or chilli

1 garlic clove, halved (optional)

Good pinch of spices or herbs (optional, see Tip)

Salt and pepper

To bake If you have the oven on for something else, at 190°C/170°C fan/gas 5 or 200°C/180°C fan/gas 6, you can bake the croutons. Brush the bread on both sides with the oil. Rub with the garlic, if using. Cut the bread into 1cm (½in) cubes, then spread over a baking tray. Add salt and pepper, and spices or herbs, if using, and toss to mix. Bake for 5–10 minutes, turning occasionally, until crisp and golden – don't let them burn. Drain on kitchen paper.

To fry Cut the bread into 1cm (½in) cubes. Heat the oil with the garlic, if using, in a frying pan over a medium-high heat – check that it's hot by adding a cube of bread: it should sizzle immediately. When hot, add the bread cubes and stir for 2–3 minutes until golden brown all over. Drain on kitchen paper and immediately sprinkle with salt and pepper, and spices or herbs, if using.

Leave to cool before storing in an airtight container in a cool, dry place for up to 5 days.

Tip

To use fresh herbs, rinse and dry well on kitchen paper, then chop finely.

Garlic Breadcrumbs

Serves **4–6**
Prep **5–10 mins**
Cook **5–10 mins**

 Vegan

The Italian name for these flavoursome breadcrumbs is *pangrattato*, sometimes known as 'poor man's Parmesan'. They are sprinkled over pasta, soups and vegetable dishes. As they can be stored in an airtight container for up to 5 days, why not make double?

3 slices slightly stale white bread, crusts removed

2 garlic cloves, very finely chopped

Pinch of chilli powder or dried chilli flakes, or grated zest of 1 lemon or 1 tbsp finely chopped fresh parsley (optional)

2 tbsp olive oil

Salt and pepper

Briefly blitz the bread in a food processor or mini chopper. Add salt and pepper, garlic, plus the flavouring, if using, to make coarse crumbs.

To bake If you have the oven on for something else, at 200°C/180°C fan/gas 6, you can bake the crumbs. Tip the crumbs onto a baking tray and drizzle over the oil, then lightly rub it in with your fingertips. Bake for 8–10 minutes, stirring halfway through, until golden and crisp – don't let them burn. Tip onto a plate and leave to cool.

To fry Heat the oil in a frying pan over a medium-high heat, add the garlicky crumbs and cook, stirring, for 4–5 minutes, until golden and crisp. Drain on kitchen paper.

Leave to cool before storing in an airtight container in a cool, dry place for up to 5 days.

Toasted Seeds

Serves   **4–6**
Prep   **20 mins,
plus cooling**
Cook   **5–15 mins**

 Vegan

GF   Gluten-free

Pumpkin, sunflower and sesame seeds are readily available, but they benefit from toasting in a dry frying pan for 2–3 minutes to bring out their nutty flavour before you sprinkle them over soup. Alternatively, make your own toasted seeds the next time you prepare a squash or pumpkin. It's a sticky business, but the reward is a tasty free snack or soup topping. The seeds crisp up as they cool, so try to avoid nibbling them while they're still warm.

Seeds and stringy fibres from 1 pumpkin, butternut or other squash

1 tbsp olive oil, vegetable oil or flavoured oil, such as garlic or chilli

Good pinch of chilli powder, or smoked paprika, ground cumin or za'atar (optional)

Salt and pepper

Put the seeds and stringy pulp in a bowl of water and swish around, rubbing to remove the pulp. (They may need a second rinse.) Put them onto a clean tea towel and pat dry.

To bake If you have the oven on for something else, at 190°C/170°C fan/gas 5 or 200°C/180°C fan/gas 6, you can bake the seeds. Spread the seeds on a baking tray, add the oil and stir to mix thoroughly. Bake for 7–12 minutes, stirring halfway through, until the seeds smell toasty and are beginning to turn golden brown – don't let them burn. Mix in salt and pepper and your choice of seasoning, and leave to cool on the baking tray.

To fry Heat the oil in a frying pan over a medium-high heat, add the seeds and cook, stirring, for 3–4 minutes until beginning to turn golden. Drain on kitchen paper. Add salt and pepper and your choice of seasonings while the seeds are hot, then leave to cool.

Store in a sealed jar in a cool, dark place for up to 2 weeks.

Dukkah

A spicy blend of nuts and seeds, dukkah is originally from Egypt. It makes a fabulous topping for soups, salads and roasted vegetables. You can also serve it as a dip, with bread and good olive oil.

Serves	**4–6**
Prep	**5 mins, plus cooling**
Cook	**5–10 mins**

 Vegan

 Gluten-free

80g (2¾oz) hazelnuts

1 tbsp coriander seeds

1 tbsp cumin seeds

1 tsp fennel seeds

2 tbsp sesame seeds

½ tsp sea salt flakes

½ tsp ground black pepper

½ tsp sweet paprika or ground cinnamon (optional)

Preheat the oven to 190°C/170°C fan/gas 5. Spread the nuts on a baking tray and bake for 5–10 minutes, shaking the tray occasionally, until they smell nutty and are beginning to turn golden brown – don't let them burn. If they're still in their skins, tip them onto a clean tea towel and rub off the skins. Leave to cool.

Meanwhile, in a small, dry frying pan, toast the seeds for 2–3 minutes until aromatic. Leave to cool.

Grind the nuts and seeds very briefly using a pestle and mortar or in a spice grinder – you're aiming for a very coarse powder with some crunchy texture. Stir in the salt and pepper, and paprika or cinnamon if using.

Store in a sealed jar in a cool, dark place for up to 1 month.

Tip

Roasting the hazelnuts in the oven seems to bring out a better nutty flavour, especially if the nuts are still in their skins, but you could toast them in a small dry frying pan, for 10–15 minutes, stirring often. Tip them out and leave to cool while you toast the remaining seeds.

Crispy Shallots

A popular topping for soups, curries and stir-fries in South-East Asia, these shallots go well with Laksa (page 70) or with soups such as potato, root vegetables, squash or lentil.

Serves **4–6**
Prep **15 mins, plus cooling**
Cook **10–15 mins**

V0 Vegan
GF Gluten-free

200g (7oz) shallots
400ml (14fl oz) vegetable oil
Salt

Slice the shallots very finely, as evenly as possible. Tip them onto a clean tea towel and gently tumble them about to remove some of the moisture. If you have time, spread them out and leave to dry for 20–30 minutes.

Pour oil into a wok or saucepan until it's about 1cm (½in) deep and put over a medium heat until the oil begins to shimmer. Add the shallots and reduce the heat so that the oil is bubbling gently but steadily. Cook for 8–10 minutes, stirring the shallots so that they cook evenly, until light golden brown – don't let them get too brown, because they will continue to brown for a minute or two off the heat.

Pour the shallots and oil into a metal sieve over a bowl, then tip the shallots onto a plate lined with kitchen paper, sprinkle with salt while they're hot and leave to cool and crisp up. (See Tip for reusing the oil.)

Once cool and crisp, store in an airtight container in a cool, dry place for up to 10 days.

Tips

- You can reuse the oil for frying or in dressings. Leave to cool, then strain through a fine sieve to catch any bits of shallot, and store in a sealed, labelled container.
- You can cook onions in the same way, but they'll take longer to cook and will have a more assertive flavour.

Crispy Chickpeas

Serves **4–6**
Prep **15 mins, plus cooling**
Cook **20 mins**

Vegan
Gluten-free

Add this super-crunchy topping to soups made with pulses, such as Roasted Carrot, Harissa and Chickpea Soup (page 75), Red Lentil, Chickpea and Fresh Coriander Soup (page 77) or Moroccan-Style Vegetable and Chicken Soup (page 94).

400g (14oz) tin chickpeas, drained and rinsed

2 tsp vegetable oil

1 tsp ground cumin

1 tsp ground coriander

Salt and pepper

Preheat the oven to 230°C/210°C fan/gas 8 and line a roasting tin with baking paper. Dry the chickpeas on a clean tea towel, cover with another tea towel and rub gently to remove the skins (these can trap moisture). Put the chickpeas into a bowl, add the oil, cumin, coriander and some salt and pepper, then mix to coat.

Tip the chickpeas into the prepared roasting tin and roast for 20 minutes or until crisp, shaking the tin once or twice. Tip onto a plate and leave to cool; they will crisp up further.

Tip

If you have any left over, crispy chickpeas make a great snack. Store in an airtight container in a cool, dry place for up to 5 days.

Veg Crisps

Serves   **4–6**
Prep   **15 mins, plus drying and cooling**
Cook   **10 mins**

V∅   Vegan
GF   Gluten-free

A fun way to avoid food waste and make a tasty snack or soup topping. Parsnips, sweet potatoes, carrots, celeriac and beetroot all work well – be sure to scrub them before peeling. Alternatively, you can use the whole vegetable, scrubbed well and cut into thin slices.

A selection of root vegetables, such as parsnip, celeriac, beetroot, carrot, sweet potato

Vegetable oil, as needed

Salt and pepper

Scrub the veg, then peel in thin strips. (Alternatively, cut the whole, scrubbed veg into very thin slices using a vegetable peeler or a mandolin. Pat them dry as thoroughly as possible – if you have time, leave them on a clean tea towel for 10–20 minutes to dry them a bit more.

Preheat the oven to 150°C/130°C fan/gas 2. Put the peel strips or veg slices in a bowl with a little oil (about 1 teaspoon for 2 large parsnips) and some salt and pepper, then rub with your fingers to ensure that all the veg is coated in the oil.

Spread the veg in a single layer on one or two large baking trays – not overlapping or they won't crisp. Bake for 15–20 minutes, turning the baking trays halfway through, until browned – but don't let them burn. Transfer to a wire rack and leave to cool and crisp up.

Don't add to your soup until just before serving or they will soften.

Potato Peel Crisps

Potatoes crisp up better when cooked at a higher temperature. Scrub the potatoes and cut out any blemishes. Peel using a vegetable peeler, then dry as above. Preheat the oven to 220°C/200°C fan/gas 7. Mix the strips of peel with a little oil (about ½ tablespoon for 2 medium potatoes) and some salt and pepper, then rub with your fingers to ensure that they are evenly coated in oil. Spread in a single layer on one or two large baking trays and bake for 12–15 minutes, turning the baking trays after 8–9 minutes, until golden brown. Watch them carefully, as they can very quickly burn. Transfer to a wire rack and leave to cool and crisp up

Kale Crisps

A delicious accompaniment to many soups based on vegetables or pulses, kale crisps are also a moreish, sort-of-healthy snack.

Serves **4**
Prep **15 mins, plus cooling**
Cook **20 mins**

 Vegan
 Gluten-free

150g (5½oz) kale

1 tbsp olive oil

Salt

Ground black pepper, or ½ tsp smoked paprika or ½ tsp garlic granules (optional)

Preheat the oven to 140°C/120°C fan/gas 1. Line two baking trays with baking paper. Wash the kale and dry thoroughly on a clean tea towel. Remove the tough stalks and ribs, and tear the leaves.

Place in a bowl, add the oil and a good pinch of salt, plus some ground black pepper or other flavouring, if using, and rub into the kale to coat thoroughly.

Spread the kale over the prepared baking trays in a single layer and bake for 10 minutes. Turn the kale, using a spatula, and return to the oven for a further 3–4 minutes or until crisp – don't let it burn. Remove from the oven and leave to cool on the trays.

Once cool, store in an airtight container in a cool, dry place for up to 24 hours. Don't add to your soup until just before serving or the kale will soften.

Prosciutto Crisps

Serves **4–6**
Prep **5 mins, plus cooling**
Cook **5–10 mins**

 Gluten-free

Use any dry-cured ham, such as Parma or serrano, to make a crisp accompaniment to asparagus, pea, melon or parsnip soup.

4 thin slices prosciutto

Preheat the oven to 180°C/160°C fan/gas 4. Line a baking sheet with baking paper. Lay the ham in a single layer on the prepared baking sheet and bake for 5 minutes.

Turn the slices over and bake for a further 2 minutes. If they are crisp (and they will crisp up a bit more as they cool), remove from the oven and leave on a plate to cool. Depending on the thickness and dryness of the ham, it may need a little longer in the oven, but keep watching and checking that it's not browning.

To serve, break the ham into large shards or small pieces, but don't add to your soup until just before serving or it will soften.

Once cool, store in an airtight container in a cool, dry place for up to 8 hours.

Parmesan Crisps

Makes **6–8**
Prep **5 mins, plus cooling**
Cook **3–4 mins**

GF Gluten-free

Light and savoury, these crisps have a delicate crunch. Serve them with vegetable soups such as asparagus, pumpkin or minestrone.

50g (1¾oz) Parmesan, grated

Tip

Use Grana Padano or a vegetarian or vegan alternative to Parmesan if you prefer.

Preheat the oven to 200°C/180°C fan/gas 6. Line a baking sheet with baking paper. Spoon tablespoons of the grated cheese onto the prepared baking sheet, spacing them well apart, then flatten them slightly.

Put in the hot oven for 3–4 minutes until bubbling and just beginning to brown at the edges. Remove from the oven and leave to cool on the baking sheet for 5 minutes. Use a palette knife to carefully transfer them to a wire rack to cool and crisp – they will be crisp within a minute or two.

Store in an airtight container in a cool, dry place for up to 3 days.

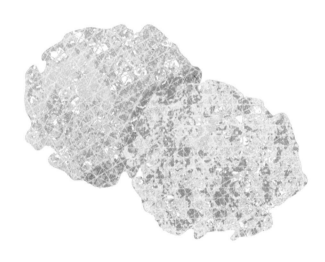

Soda Bread

Serves **6–8**
Prep **15 mins, plus cooling**
Cook **20–25 mins**

 Vegan

This beautiful homemade bread can be on the table in under an hour with very little effort and no waiting for the dough to rise. If you have any left over, it's very good toasted the next day.

250ml (9fl oz) soya milk

1 tbsp white wine vinegar or lemon juice

170g (6oz) wholemeal flour

170g (6oz) self-raising flour

½ tsp bicarbonate of soda

½ tsp salt

Preheat the oven to 200°C/180°C fan/gas 6. Line a baking sheet with baking paper.

Measure the soya milk into a jug, add the vinegar and stir well. Set aside.

Put the wholemeal flour into a large mixing bowl, then sift in the self-raising flour, bicarbonate of soda and salt, and stir to mix.

Make a well in the centre, add the soya milk mixture and mix until just combined and there are no dry bits. Dust your work surface with flour and knead the dough very lightly to bring the mixture together; the dough should be soft but not sticky. Put on the prepared baking sheet and use a large sharp knife to cut a cross in the top of the dough.

Bake for 20–25 minutes: the bread is ready if it sounds hollow when you tap the bottom of the loaf. Cool on a wire rack for 10 minutes before slicing.

Cheddar Scones

Makes **6**
Prep **20 mins**
Cook **15–20 mins**

 Vegetarian

If you don't have a sweet tooth, a savoury scone makes a welcome addition to afternoon tea – or enjoy it, while still slightly warm, alongside a bowl of soup.

Vegetable oil, for greasing

225g (8oz) self-raising flour, plus extra for dusting

½ tsp baking powder

55g (2oz) soft margarine, or chilled butter, cut into small cubes

½ tsp English mustard powder (optional)

115g (4oz) mature Cheddar cheese, grated

About 150ml (5fl oz) milk, plus extra for brushing

Salt and cayenne pepper

Preheat the oven to 220°C/200°C fan/gas 7. Lightly oil a baking sheet.

Sift the flour, baking powder and a pinch of salt into a bowl. Add the margarine and rub in using your fingertips. Stir in the mustard powder (if using), a pinch of cayenne and most of the cheese, reserving a little of the cheese for topping the scones.

Gradually stir the milk into the flour to make a soft, but not sticky, dough: you may not need all the milk.

Turn out onto a floured surface, knead lightly until smooth, then roll out to about 2.5cm (1in) thick. Use a 7.5cm (3in) round cutter to stamp out your scones, taking care not to twist the cutter, and place them on the prepared baking sheet. Very lightly knead the trimmings together and stamp out one or two more scones.

Brush the tops lightly with milk, then sprinkle with the reserved cheese, pressing it down lightly. Bake for 15–20 minutes until well risen and golden brown. Cool on a wire rack.

Cornbread Muffins

These lightly spicy golden muffins are best eaten on the day they're made. Serve them with Gumbo (page 122), Caldo Verde (page 20) or Black Bean Soup (page 66).

4 tbsp vegetable oil, plus extra for brushing (optional)

200g (7oz) gluten-free self-raising flour

1 tsp baking powder

Pinch of salt

85g (3oz) fine polenta

¼ tsp chilli flakes (optional)

2 tbsp finely chopped fresh parsley (optional)

2 eggs

200ml (7fl oz) milk

1 heaped tbsp pumpkin seeds

Preheat the oven to 200°C/180°C fan/gas 6. Brush 6 holes of a non-stick muffin tin thoroughly with oil, or line with paper cases.

Sift the flour, baking powder and salt into a bowl, add the polenta and the chilli flakes, if using, and mix well, then stir in the parsley.

In a bowl or jug, whisk together the eggs, milk and oil, then pour into the dry ingredients and stir until just mixed.

Spoon the mixture into the muffin cases and sprinkle with pumpkin seeds. Bake for 15–20 minutes or until risen and springy to the touch. Cool on a wire rack.

Tips

- When mixing in the eggs and milk you could add one or more of the following: 4 finely chopped spring onions; 50g (1¾oz) defrosted frozen (or drained tinned) sweetcorn kernels; 100g (3½oz) grated Cheddar or smoked Cheddar; and if not vegetarian, 100g (3½oz) streaky bacon, cooked until crisp, then drained.
- Once you have filled the muffin cases, get them into the oven as soon as possible because the raising agents start to work as soon as the liquid is added.

Parmesan Biscuits

Makes **about 20 small biscuits**

Prep **20 mins, plus chilling and cooling**

Cook **10 mins**

Buttery, crumbly and irresistibly moreish, these little biscuits are perfect with a variety of vegetable soups – from asparagus to vichyssoise.

70g (2½oz) plain flour

70g (2½oz) butter, cut into small cubes

70g (2½oz) Parmesan, finely grated

1 tsp finely chopped fresh rosemary leaves or 1 tsp dried oregano

Vegetable oil, for greasing

1 egg, beaten

Caraway, cumin, nigella, poppy or sesame seeds, to sprinkle

Salt and pepper

Sift the flour and a pinch of salt into a bowl. Add the butter and rub in using your fingertips. Stir in the Parmesan, rosemary or oregano and a grinding of black pepper. Press the mixture together to form a dough. Alternatively, put the ingredients into a food processor and pulse until the mixture clumps together.

Shape into a long roll about 3cm (1¼in) in diameter. Wrap in baking paper and chill for 1 hour or overnight.

Preheat the oven to 180°C/160°C fan/gas 4. Lightly oil a baking sheet.

Slice the dough into 5mm (¼in) thick rounds and place on the prepared baking sheet. Brush with beaten egg and sprinkle the top with your choice of seeds. Bake for 10 minutes or until golden. Leave to cool on the baking sheet for 5 minutes, then transfer to a wire rack to cool completely.

Store in an airtight container in a cool, dry place for up to 3 days.

Tips

- Instead of Parmesan, you could use mature Cheddar or another well-flavoured hard cheese.
- Keep any leftover beaten egg in a small sealed container in the fridge for up to 3 days or in the freezer for up to 3 months to use next time you need egg to glaze.

Index

Note: page numbers in **bold**
refer to recipe illustrations.

175

Acknowledgements

Many thanks to David Salmo and Peter Taylor at HarperCollins for their support and heroic patience. Love and hugs to Nikki, aka the extraordinary cook Nichola J Taylor (@incabellablog), for ideas, advice and encouragement in so many ways. Special thanks to John Gingell, supergenius, and to Ian Chilvers, who regularly sends chocolate to make sure I have a balanced diet. Above all, love and thanks to Andrew Fyvie, sculptor, chief taster and domestic martyr.